H. Richard Lamb, *University of Southern California*
EDITOR-IN-CHIEF

Best of *New Directions for Mental Health Services,* 1979–2001

H. Richard Lamb
University of Southern California

EDITOR

Number 91, Fall 2001

JOSSEY-BASS
A Wiley Company
www.josseybass.com

BEST OF NEW DIRECTIONS FOR MENTAL HEALTH SERVICES, 1979–2001
H. Richard Lamb (ed.)
New Directions for Mental Health Services, no. 91
H. Richard Lamb, Editor-in-Chief

Microfilm copies of issues and articles are available in 16mm and 35mm, as well as microfiche in 105mm, through University Microfilms Inc., 300 North Zeeb Road, Ann Arbor, Michigan 48106-1346.

ISSN 0193-9416   ISBN 0-7879-1440-1

NEW DIRECTIONS FOR MENTAL HEALTH SERVICES is part of The Jossey-Bass Psychology Series and is published quarterly by Jossey-Bass Inc., Publishers, 350 Sansome Street, San Francisco, California 94104-1342.

SUBSCRIPTIONS cost $66.00 for individuals and $121.00 for institutions, agencies, and libraries.

EDITORIAL CORRESPONDENCE should be sent to the Editor-in-Chief, H. Richard Lamb, University of Southern California, Department of Psychiatry, Graduate Hall, 1937 Hospital Place, Los Angeles, California 90033–1071.

Cover photograph by Wernher Krutein/PHOTOVAULT ©1990.

Jossey-Bass Web address: www.josseybass.com

Printed in the United States of America on acid-free recycled paper containing 100 percent recovered waste paper, of which at least 20 percent is postconsumer waste.

CONTENTS

Editor's Notes

In 1978, the late Allen Jossey-Bass, founder of Jossey-Bass Publishers, asked me to edit a new series, titled *New Directions for Mental Health Services*. I was not terribly interested, but Allen was a charismatic person with remarkable charm, and I finally agreed to do it for a year or two. Now twenty-two years and ninety-one issues later, I am doing my last issue. I am told that I have far and away broken all longevity records for *New Directions* series editors, and in fact, I have enjoyed editing all of the issues—well, almost all. However, I feel that it is now time to move on to other things, so this will be the last issue under my editorship.

How to end it? After considering a number of possibilities, I have chosen nine chapters from the series on the basis of various criteria— some because they presented an important new perspective or conceptual advance that made a significant contribution to the field, some because they represent the thinking of one of the leading persons in our profession, some because they express a point of view that most would be fearful of putting in print, and some because they are just superb practical and clinical chapters. Some meet several of these criteria. What they all have in common is that I was excited when I first read them, they are interesting and well written, they contributed something of importance to the field, they are still relevant, there is something of significance to be learned from them, and from a subjective point of view, I enjoy rereading them.

The chapters are presented in the order in which they appeared. The chapter by Bert Pepper, Hilary Ryglewicz, and Michael Kirshner, The Uninstitutionalized Generation, published in Bert Pepper's and Hilary Ryglewicz's 1982 issue, *The Young Adult Chronic Patient*, made us aware that deinstitutionalization had resulted in a new generation of psychiatrically disabled young adults that presented new and different problems and demanded new and different solutions. This was a consequence of deinstitutionalization that no one had anticipated.

The lead chapter by Kenneth Minkoff in his 1991 issue, *Dual Diagnosis of Major Mental Illness and Substance Disorder*, coedited with Robert Drake, addressed another major problem of deinstitutionalization. It described those persons dually diagnosed with severe mental illness and substance use disorders and presented in a comprehensive manner a range of ways to conceptualize the problem and to treat and rehabilitate this challenging group.

The chapter by Nancy Atwood, Combining Individual and Family Treatment: Guidelines for the Therapist, published in David Greenfeld's 1992 issue, *Treating Diverse Disorders with Psychotherapy*, is a high-quality guide, illustrated with case examples, for combining individual and family treatment for severely mentally ill persons. It is at the same time unusually insightful and practical and is extremely valuable to clinicians attempting to treat persons with severe mental illness.

In my opinion, Jerry Dincin is—and has been over the years—the most thoughtful and progressive person in psychiatric rehabilitation, and this was reflected in his 1995 issue, *A Pragmatic Approach to Psychiatric Rehabilitation: Lessons from Chicago's Thresholds Program*. Although a number of chapters could have been chosen from this volume, I have selected The Biological Basis of Mental Illness, which addresses a number of issues that are seldom put into print so clearly in the literature on psychosocial rehabilitation.

Few nonforensic mental health professionals have a clear idea of what they should do in court as an expert witness, and few forensic mental health professionals are able to clearly tell them. Steven Bank's 1996 article from Elissa Benedek's issue, *Emerging Issues in Forensic Psychiatry: From the Clinic to the Courthouse*, is an exception and a pleasure to read.

The family movement has been a major advance in our field and along with it the development and conceptualization of interventions for family members with a seriously mentally ill relative. Phyllis Solomon's chapter in Harriet Lefley's 1998 issue, *Families Coping with Mental Illness: The Cultural Context*, clearly describes the various kinds of interventions and their significance and makes an excellent introduction to a fine volume.

What if any is the place of spirituality and religion in mental health services? Roger Fallot's chapter in his 1998 issue, *Spirituality and Religion in Recovery from Mental Illness*, gives us some much needed answers to this question that many mental health professionals have tended to avoid. Ironically, many seriously mentally ill persons place a high value on spirituality, which appears to be of great help to them. This chapter and this issue have helped to update our field.

No one in our field has written so insightfully and has had such an impact on our thinking about and understanding of the effects and implications of every aspect of deinstitutionalization than Leona Bachrach. In her chapter in William Spaulding's 1999 issue, *The Role of the State Hospital in the Twenty-First Century*, she illuminates, as no one else has, the thorny issues that surround any discussion of the subject of the state mental hospital.

Violence is an extremely important problem in our society generally. Mental health is no exception. If we are to deal with violence and ideally prevent it, we must do what is necessary to feel safe. When this subject is discussed, there usually is a tendency to fall back on political correctness and soft-pedal the issues. Not so in the chapter on clinician safety by Arthur Berg, Carl Bell, and Joe Tupin in Carl Bell's 2000 issue, *Psychiatric Aspects of Violence: Issues in Prevention and Treatment*. This chapter describes in a straightforward manner the problem and ways of dealing with it. For that matter, the entire issue is an important contribution to the literature.

I hope you enjoy reading or rereading these chapters as much as I did.

H. Richard Lamb
Editor

H. RICHARD LAMB *is professor of psychiatry and the behavioral sciences at Keck School of Medicine, University of Southern California in Los Angeles.*

Our first generation of young adult chronic psychiatric patients since deinstitutionalization has emerged in the community. Updated research results and case studies show different patterns of emergence but similar indications for clinician response.

The Uninstitutionalized Generation: A New Breed of Psychiatric Patient

Bert Pepper, Hilary Ryglewicz, Michael C. Kirshner

Who is the *young adult chronic patient?* This unsatisfactory phrase, which has spread from Rockland County into the professional language, is used to describe a generation of young adults in the age group eighteen to thirty-five who are now living in our communities but who show persistent and severe impairment in their psychological and social functioning. They are young persons who, as they grow older, require services from mental health and other social agencies in a variety of ways and over a period of years. We have called them an emerging, uninstitutionalized generation; many of them are persons who in the past would have become long-stay patients in mental institutions or at the least would have had one or several hospitalizations of one or more years' duration. Today, however, they spend little if any time in our psychiatric institutions. The seriously emotionally disturbed person who has become ill in the past fifteen or twenty years usually can measure his or her total length of stay in state institutions and other hospitals in weeks or months rather than in years and decades. Even the schizophrenic patient who has been hospitalized three times in the past ten years probably has spent perhaps 12 months in hospitals, and 108 months in the community. These young adults, then, are our first generation of chronic psychiatric patients to grow up in community care and in the wake of the great wave of deinstitutionalization and its corollaries: admissions diversion, tightened involuntary admission criteria, and the limitations of hospital stays to the briefest possible time.

Many of these patients are diagnosed schizophrenic, and many others carry a diagnosis of other major mental or personality disorder. Many are multiply diagnosed—especially since the advent of DSM-III (*Diagnostic and*

Statistical Manual of Mental Disorders, Third Edition, 1980)—with symptoms of mental illness superimposed on an underlying personality disorder. But our view of this patient group cuts across diagnostic lines, for our focus is on the functional disabilities of these young persons.

We may note here that the term *disability* itself refers to functioning, in this case functioning in the social context of a community (Gruenberg, 1974). The pathology of intrapsychic functioning, which constitutes an impairment that we may call mental illness or personality disorder, may not result in a disability in terms of living in a mental institution or being cared for as a dependent child in the context of one's family. But these impairments do constitute disabilities when the young adult attempts to become independent and self-supporting, to leave the protection of the family, to make stable relationships, and to live normally as a member of the community.

The constellation of symptoms that Gruenberg described two decades ago as *social breakdown syndrome* (poor social and psychological functioning, apathy, negativism, and docility mingled with episodic outbursts) was once seen, in part, as the product of the patient's interaction with the institutional environment—which was dull, understimulating, limited, predictable, protective, directive, and authoritarian (Gruenberg, 1963; Gruenberg, Brandon, and Kasius, 1966; Goffman, 1962). Today we see cases of social breakdown syndrome in the community context (Gruenberg and others, 1972; Gruenberg, 1974)—an environment that by contrast is exciting, overstimulating, open, unpredictable, dangerous, confusing, and demanding of choices by patients. The intrapsychic pathology of our young adult patients has not changed, but its expression has changed through their interaction with the community. Our problems with patients and responsibilities for their care are now different as well.

As caregivers, we find in young adult chronic patients the bane and despair of our working lives. Typically, they make poor use—underuse, overuse, misuse, abuse—of the services that are available. As perhaps 10 percent of our patient population, they consume perhaps 40 percent of our staff time. They tend not to define themselves as mental patients and do not have, unlike their older, long-institutionalized counterparts, years of training in doing as they are told (Segal, Baumohl, and Johnson, 1977; Segal and Baumohl, 1980). Instead they want to be treated—and to act out—in the manner of their peers. They leave us as they leave their parents: with optimism or defiance, only to return again in crisis. They are typically our emergencies, our unexplained terminations, our no-shows, our unscheduled sessions, and our AMA (against-medical-advice) discharges. In a system such as Rockland County's, their charts are thick and have many sections, notes from several programs and clinicians, many beginnings and premature endings, and often two or three scribbled suicide notes. They are frustrating, difficult to treat, and often too withdrawn or disruptive to be readily engaged in treatment.

It may be too pessimistic to refer to all of these young persons as chronically disabled, although the phrase is accurate for many in the context of our present resources for treatment and support. These are the patients we may think of as our failures; certainly, failure is the most common element in their experience. They begin jobs, only to lose them; they begin school, only to drop out; they begin relationships, only to suffer additional conflict, dependency, and disappointment. Many try in vain to separate from their parents but continually fall back into their reluctant embrace, seeking shelter, support, sustenance; many virtually withdraw from efforts to make it in the world; and many are engaged with their families in a repetitive cycle of hope, fear, rage, shame, and the current violent conflict of prisoners locked together in a room with no exit.

If we look at these dysfunctional young adults in developmental terms, they seem to be stuck in the transition to adult life, unable to master the tasks of separation and independence. If we examine the nature of their failures, we find them to be based on more or less severe and chronic pathology: thought disorder; affective disorder; personality disorder; and severe deficits in ego functions such as impulse control, reality testing, judgment, modulation of affect, memory, mastery and competence, and integration. In terms of the necessary equipment for community life—the capacity to endure stress, to work consistently toward realistic goals, to relate to other people comfortably over time, to tolerate uncertainty and conflict—these young adults are disabled in a very real and pervasive sense.

Case Histories

Let us briefly introduce to your imagination three such young adults. These are all real persons, and their cases are not unusual.

1. Sam is an attractive, curly-haired young man of twenty-seven, whose poor self-image shows in his posture and his expression: his head is slightly lowered, his body is poised as if for "fight or flight," and his look is mistrustful, a blend of sullenness and anxiety. Sam's problems did not emerge until late in high school, when he began using drugs and showed some personality change, becoming "belligerent and uncooperative." He first came to our crisis service at the age of eighteen, complaining, "I think I'm a moron." He had already attempted suicide more than once, usually under the influence of alcohol. He had a girlfriend but felt unable to relate to her. He was still living at home with his parents—described as chronically in conflict, with Sam caught in the middle. He already had a history of drug abuse, smoking marijuana at times and experiencing paranoid episodes when he took LSD. He was disorganized, preoccupied with daydreams, and concerned that he might be homosexual.

In the nine years following this episode, Sam has had seven psychiatric hospitalizations for anxiety, depression, confusion, and paranoid delusions;

he has had multiple contacts with our crisis service and several referrals to our outpatient clinics. He has been treated at our acute day treatment program, referred to a vocational rehabilitation workshop, and placed at a residential farm for psychiatric patients, which he had to leave because of drinking. He has gone away to college but dropped out to return home; he has begun jobs but lost them because he would lie in bed in the morning. He has repeatedly been diagnosed schizophrenic and put on medication but has repeatedly stopped his medications and dropped out of treatment. He has continually returned to use of alcohol and marijuana, usually in connection with his efforts to make friends.

2. Nick is a tall, thin, shy twenty-one-year-old, who says he feels "like a jerk." He was born with a blood disease that necessitated a complete transfusion at birth. His family background includes an older brother who was hospitalized for psychiatric illness at an early age. Nick was in special classes from first grade until high school graduation, showing a dull-normal full-scale IQ with mild visual-motor problems and severe, chronic feelings of inferiority. Since his parents' marital conflict culminated in divorce, he has been living with his father, who also appears depressed and withdrawn. Nick is diagnosed as mixed personality disorder with schizoid, paranoid, and avoidant features. He has been attending social and vocational rehabilitation programs since high school but still has great difficulty making social relationships. He was hospitalized recently when he became depressed about his future and tried to cut his wrists with the wires of his orthodontic braces.

3. Nancy is a bright, bouncy, outspoken young woman of twenty-four, who was able to complete two years of college and has had a few periods of successful work history as a therapy aide. She is cheerful, affectionate, likable, full of fun, and full of life. She is also, at times, volatile, impatient, disruptive, profane, threatening, grandiose, and impulsive. She has had four psychiatric hospitalizations and is on lithium for manic-depressive illness, with an additional diagnosis of passive-aggressive personality. Nancy has abused drugs since age thirteen, starting with marijuana, glue sniffing, cocaine and amphetamines, and more recently including alcohol. Her problems in maintaining steady employment have resulted in severe financial crises, and her manic episodes have involved disastrous conflicts with landlords. Yet her intelligence and some successful work history make it very difficult for her to accept any lowering of her standard of living or of her hopes about the future. At present, she is living in a transitional apartment and struggling to overcome her habitual use of drugs, which seems to play a part in precipitating her manic episodes.

These three young adults provide an idea of the range and variety of symptoms presented by our patient group, yet their social and treatment needs are in many ways strikingly similar. The most crippling aspects of their mental disorders are the effects of those disorders on the social functioning of these young persons and on their use, nonuse, or misuse of opportunities for treatment. When we strip away the pressure-sensitive diagnostic labels, their essential problem is that they cannot seem to get or keep anything positive going in their lives, including therapy.

In view of this, at the Rockland County Community Mental Health Center (CMHC) we have been pursuing a course of investigation designed to provide more data about young adult patients who show persistent difficulties in psychological and social functioning. We are also trying to develop a more precise understanding of the various routes by which these patients come to our attention, and the ages and stages at which they develop dysfunctional behavior.

The center is the core agency of a unified services network that embraces the total care and treatment system for mentally ill, mentally retarded, developmentally disabled, alcoholic, and drug-abusing residents of our county of 270,000 persons. This large organization offers a natural habitat for studying young adults who are chronically mentally ill or socially disabled and for observing them in a variety of treatment programs.

We began with a very modest initial study of a segment of our own treatment population. From a group of 900 young adults in the age group eighteen to thirty who were seen at any of our six outpatient clinics within a three-month period in 1980, we identified, through input from clinicians and chart review, a group of nearly 300 who could be categorized as young adult chronic patients. This categorization was based on the severe and persistent nature of their disabilities and their dysfunctional use of treatment. Of these nearly 300 persons

- 55 percent were male and 45 percent were female;
- 55 percent had mental health treatment before age eighteen;
- 25 percent had never been hospitalized;
- 60 percent were unemployed;
- 30 percent were receiving federal social security income based on disability;
- 27 percent were on public assistance;
- 19 percent were receiving support from their families; and only
- 24 percent were self-supporting;
- 24 percent were known to have been in trouble with the law;
- 37 percent had a known history of alcohol abuse, and 37 percent (not necessarily the same 37 percent) had a known history of marijuana abuse;
- 28 percent had a known history of other drug abuse; and for
- 42 percent of these persons, suicide had been an issue addressed in treatment.

We are now engaged in a more extensive effort to explore the size, nature, and needs of Rockland County's young adult chronic patient population. Of 1,200 young adults who had at least one contact with our center in 1980 and at least one contact two years or more before, 800 were seen by their most recent clinicians as having the characteristics that define this patient group. We are now in the process of evaluating results of a questionnaire filled out by the clinicians of a sample of 250 of these 800 young adult chronic patients and those of a control group of nonchronic young adults. Although the data must be verified through further analysis, preliminary results from a subsample of 100 of the chronic group suggest that

- 69 percent had mental health treatment before age eighteen (47 percent outpatient, 22 percent inpatient).
- 55 percent are known by their clinicians to have used or abused alcohol or other drugs, or a combination of both.
- 10 percent are known to have been involved in a criminal offense with violence.
- 5 percent are known to have been involved in a criminal offense without violence.
- 45 percent are still living with their families.
- 22 percent have their own children living with them, ranging in age from two to seventeen (for this group of 100 young adult patients, there were forty-four such children living with their [twenty-two] parents).
- 31 percent are supported totally by some form of public assistance (including Supplemental Security Income [SSI]).
- 8 percent receive public assistance supplementing part-time employment.
- 32 percent are supported by either parents or spouse or both.
- 22 percent are self-supporting.
- 35 percent have made suicide attempts.

As noted elsewhere in this journal, the high suicide rate characteristic of this patient group becomes even more alarming when a city population is considered (Caton, 1981).

Based on both this developing exploratory study and our clinical observations of the young adult chronically disabled population, we would like to focus attention on two aspects of this patient group: first, the process of development of their problems; and second, the process of their identification and treatment.

Evolution of the Problems

Our studies suggest that a majority of the young adult chronic patient population had received treatment before age eighteen. For some, like Nick, this means that problems were evident in childhood and that some form of intervention was made even within the elementary school years. For others, the breakdown in functioning began in the adolescent years, sometimes in conjunction with the use of marijuana, alcohol, or other drugs as a part of recreational activity with peers. Our studies indicate that a majority of these young adults have a history of alcohol and marijuana abuse. There is some evidence accumulating that even brief use of marijuana may be a precipitating factor in psychotic episodes of persons who may be predisposed to develop psychiatric disorder.

Certainly, it is observable in our own inpatient population that rehospitalizations often occur following ingestion of drugs. This becomes a thorny issue in treatment for our young adult chronic patients, who prefer to see these symptoms as a temporary reaction to drug use and may say, "I used some bad stuff" or "Somebody slipped something into my drink," and yet strongly resist any implication that the recreational use of drugs enjoyed by their peers is off-limits for them. Not only do they resist the idea that they are different and must observe a restriction because of a chronic vulnerability to certain kinds of stimuli, but many also find, in their use of drugs, their only respite from the demands of reality and their only means of enjoying a commonality or making an effort to socialize with others of their age.

We do not know at this point what chemical interactions may be involved in the vulnerability to marijuana of young persons who have an underlying disorder that emerges in psychosis. But considering the issue only in terms of ego functions, we can certainly surmise that drug use becomes abuse for young persons who have not been able to achieve other kinds of gratifications and that a vicious cycle then ensues. The repeated retreat into drugs prevents the development of other satisfactions through goal-directed activity and also prevents the working out of other issues, such as the capacity to handle feelings of frustration, low self-esteem, and interpersonal conflict.

There is another and, again, very large group of young adult chronic patients whose breakdown in functioning appears only as the individual comes of age and attempts to separate from parents and to achieve autonomy. As we have noted before, the patient is stuck in the process of transition to adulthood. For some, functioning has been at least adequate through the high school years, but a breakdown has followed the attempt to go away to college, to marry, or to live with a girlfriend or boyfriend, and in particular, to become self-supporting—that is, to hold a job through consistent work activity. At this point, for many young persons, the personality structure proves inadequate to the new tasks of maturation into responsible adulthood. We know that young adulthood is often the time of the "first break" in schizophrenia. We are now seeing an apparent increase in the diagnosis of manic-depressive illness (bipolar disorder) in young persons, rather than the more typical picture of a manic disorder emerging in midlife. Again, we cannot say to what extent this seeming increase reflects an increased sensitivity to symptoms of mood disorder on the part of diagnosticians (following upon the availability and popularity of lithium) or an actual increase in emergence of the disorder at this earlier stage of life. The case of Nancy, whose use of drugs has become an increasingly obvious precipitant to her manic episodes, suggests a need for further research into the ramifications of the use of street drugs in the presence of a chronic chemical imbalance.

In the case of Sam (who apparently functioned well through high school but showed a personality change at the time he became involved with drugs), we also do not know whether the functional change and the drug use were two reflections of the same difficulty—a breakdown in ego functions when confronting the tasks of separation and autonomy. It may be that the personality change and the development of severe anxiety and self-doubt were in fact secondary to the effects of drug use on a vulnerable individual with an underlying psychiatric disorder. As Sam has continued his course of multiple hospitalizations, his use of drugs and alcohol has presented an important element in the sabotage of efforts at rehabilitation—in one instance resulting in his discharge from a rehabilitative community.

The only other rural rehabilitative residences available for Sam would be those that focus on drug rehabilitation, which not only would be inappropriate for his needs but also would demand a level of ego strength that he does not possess. He therefore falls between two chairs, as do many of the young adults whose dual (psychiatric and substance abuse) diagnoses make them unwelcome referrals to many programs and also deserving of the term *multiply handicapped*.

Interactions with Treatment Programs

Having made these anecdotal observations of some of our young adult chronic patients, along with clinical impressions of their process of entry into patienthood, we ask the question, what about the process of their interaction with treatment programs? Here, too, if we take not only a still shot but also a movie, we see an initial episode of symptom development, whether in childhood or adolescence or young adulthood, which has an impact on family interactions and commonly results in treatment, either in the form of hospitalization or through outpatient programs. This first intervention, usually in a crisis, occurs in a context of maximum motivation and maximum optimism. Certainly, the episode comes as a shock to the young person and his or her significant others. But one episode is very different from six; the assumption, often encouraged by us as professionals, is that functioning will be restored and even improved, and we often emphasize the advantage of this early warning signal, a sign that changes are needed in the lifestyle and family interactions of the young person—and of course that therapy is indicated. The patient, too, tends to take an optimistic view at this early stage; unfortunately, much of the optimism is founded on denial. It is difficult to say, "This is what happened to me"; it feels better to say, "But it will never happen again." Often the wish to forget it ever happened leads to a failure to follow through on therapy once the crisis or hospitalization is over. This may be as true of the family as of the patient. (Sam's mother, for instance, remains convinced that all of his troubles resulted from medicine he was given at our hospital.)

But by the second or third episode, especially if hospitalization is involved, it becomes more and more difficult to take an optimistic view of the future, both for the patient and for family and staff involved in his or her care. At this point, a growing pessimism among staff and family, as well as anger and resentment on some level, and a growing despair on the part of the patient become strong negative forces in the treatment picture. We might call this a rejection phase: the family and treatment staff reject the patient; the patient rejects himself or herself as well as those who try to help. Occasionally, we have the ultimate self-rejection, suicide, sometimes as the culmination of a postpsychotic depression and sometimes resulting from an existential crisis and confrontation with a future devoid of hope.

Our therapeutic task as this process unfolds is to encourage enough recognition of the seriousness of the socially disabling disorder to motivate the patient and the family to follow through with treatment and at the same time to mitigate the despair that sometimes accompanies this recognition. We want the patient and those around the patient to feel, on the one hand, that this is a very serious problem that needs attention but, on the other, that there is still hope. Achieving this balance is a delicate task of therapy. Helping patients and their families, as well as clinicians, have appropriate expectations—not too much and not too little—is a still more delicate and equally necessary task. A striking feature of our young adult chronically disabled patients in the community is the discrepancy between the fantasy of what they would like to be able to do and the reality of what they have done and are likely to do in the future; it is the gap between the ideal of being "just like anybody else" and the reality of being unable to make anything work for very long.

Realistic Goals and Expectations

What goals can we realistically have for these dysfunctional young adults, which we can help them identify and share with us as therapists? And once (ideally) agreeing on appropriate goals, how can we tailor our treatment programs to move toward their realization?

Based on our observations of these patients, we can say that the following may be appropriate goals, both for individual clinicians and as the thrust or message of our treatment programs.

First, we must help them become more self-aware and able to identify their own early warning signals of stress and impending chaos. Working toward this kind of self-awareness is not a matter of insight therapy; it is a sensitization to one's own signals. These signals may be behaviors, affective states, or cognitive patterns. For one individual, self-awareness may mean learning to say, "When I begin to have difficulty sleeping at night, it means that something is wrong." For another, it may mean, "When I start wanting to take on the whole world at once or thinking about becoming a rock star, I'm getting out of reality"; for another, "When I begin smoking a joint, when I feel anxious, I'm headed for trouble."

The second step in this kind of self-awareness is to identify something to do about these signals of overstress or impending decompensation. Calling one's therapist is one obvious response. Staying away from people who create stress or who present the temptation to fall back into drug and alcohol abuse is another. Moving to a less upsetting environment temporarily, but not running away completely, is another. Focusing on the performance of certain daily tasks, practicing relaxation or meditation techniques, or seeking out a trusted friend or relative are yet other ways of responding. The goal is to learn ways of achieving some degree of control over the kinds of stress and the kinds of temptation that have led in the past to a breakdown of functioning and a sense of helplessness.

A third aspect of self-awareness is the focusing of attention on certain core or repetitive problems, patterns of behavior that are dysfunctional and repeatedly lead the person into trouble. Examples are brooding about real or imaginary slights, procrastinating, or deciding after two weeks on a job that it is not the right job instead of sticking with it for the sake of sticking with something and overcoming the constant temptation to give up and run away.

Clearly, we are talking here about rather basic ego functions and elementary forms of everyday behavior. For many of these young adults, the therapist and the therapeutic group have to function as a borrowed ego to help with the functions of judgment, reality testing, memory, mastery and competence, and integration. This need is really at the core of our treatment of the young adult chronic patient. These young persons are like an organism that lacks the resources of the healthy human body. They are intensely vulnerable to the stresses of daily life because they do not have the ego strength to mobilize resistance to stress, to remember and integrate life experience, and to hold on to goals and intentions that are reality based. The difficulty in mobilizing resources is not only psychological; it also interferes with patients' development of a social support network and with the constructive and appropriate use of treatment. Our first task, then, is to help them develop their own ability and willingness to utilize help and support that is available. In the absence of both inner resources and the ability and willingness to use social supports, these young persons can only retreat under stress into patterns of withdrawal, drug abuse, fear, and rage.

A fourth and related aspect of self-awareness that these young persons need to develop is the focusing on realistic short-term expectations and goals. These patients need what we, as their clinicians, need: to be able to take satisfaction in limited, step-by-step achievements; to be able to say, "I've held on to this job for three weeks, and next week it will be four weeks," instead of "This job isn't getting me anywhere, and what I want to do is get a Ph.D. in psychology and help people." The other side of the coin of unrealistic and grandiose goals is, of course, the recognition of the goal as impossibly remote and the despair of seeing reality as empty of hope and possibility. The one-day-at-a-time philosophy that has been so helpful in the treatment of alcohol addiction must become the focus of work with patients who are chronically tempted to run out on reality—if not into drugs, then into some other form of escape.

The issues just noted are examples, on the level of everyday life and everyday clinical management, of the ones we need to address with these persistently disabled young persons. What stands out as we try to address them in our treatment programs is that the same difficulties in continuity that these young persons show in their social functioning are an aspect of, and often a fatal stumbling block in, their behavior as clients and their response to treatment. It is nearly impossible to help them develop self-awareness, integration, and a sense of progress and continuity if we do not have the opportunity to work with them consistently over time and if our contacts typically take place in emergency rooms or in a ten-day stay on an inpatient unit, followed by months of no contact.

This is the problem with which we are all struggling as we try to meet the needs of the chronic young adult psychiatric patient. Our community human services networks are facing major difficulties in ensuring not only an adequate level of continuity of care but also the basic conditions of a tolerable life. Once basic needs are met, developing the capacity to provide useful treatment and support emerges as the major mental health challenge of the 1980s.

References

Caton, C.L.M. "The New Chronic Patient and the System of Community Care." *Hospital and Community Psychiatry*, 1981, *32*(7), 475–478.

Diagnostic and Statistical Manual of Mental Disorders, Third Edition. Washington, D.C.: American Psychiatric Association, 1980.

Goffman, E. *Asylums: Essays on the Social Situation of Mental Patients and Other Inmates*. New York: Doubleday, 1962.

Gruenberg, E. M. "On the Pathogenesis of the Social Breakdown Syndrome." In Mammerborn (ed.), *A Critical Review of Treatment Progress in a State Hospital Reorganized Toward the Communities Served: Treatment Programs Present and Planned, of the Colorado State Hospital*. Pueblo, Colo.: Colorado State Hospital, 1963, 96–108 (mimeograph).

Gruenberg, E. M. "The Social Breakdown Syndrome and Its Prevention." In G. Caplan (ed.), *American Handbook of Psychiatry (Volume II): Child and Adolescent Psychiatry, Sociocultural and Community Psychiatry*. (2nd ed.) New York: Basic Books, 1974.

Gruenberg, E. M., Brandon, S., and Kasius, R. V. "Identifying Cases of the Social Breakdown Syndrome." *Milbank Memorial Fund Quarterly*, Jan. 1966 (part 2), *44*, 150–155.

Gruenberg, E. M., and others. "Social Breakdown Syndrome: Environmental and Host Factors Associated with Chronicity." *American Journal of Public Health*, 1972, *62*, 91–94.

Segal, S. P., and Baumohl, J. "Engaging the Disengaged: Proposals on Madness and Vagrancy." *Social Work*, 1980, *25*(5), 358–365.

Segal, S. P., Baumohl, J., and Johnson, E. "Falling Through the Cracks: Mental Disorder and Social Margin in a Young Vagrant Population." *Social Problems*, 1977, *24*(3), 387–400.

BERT PEPPER is executive director of The Information Exchange, Inc., clinical professor of psychiatry at New York University School of Medicine, and lecturer in psychiatry at Massachusetts Mental Health Center/Harvard.

HILARY RYGLEWICZ was coordinator of family services at the Rockland County (New York) Department of Mental Health. She is now in private practice.

MICHAEL C. KIRSHNER is a psychologist at the Rockland County (New York) Department of Mental Health.

2

Using an integrated theoretical framework, a continuous and comprehensive model system of care for dual diagnosis patients can be designed.

Program Components of a Comprehensive Integrated Care System for Seriously Mentally Ill Patients with Substance Disorders

Kenneth Minkoff

During the last two decades, deinstitutionalization has been increasingly associated with the emergence of large numbers of individuals with concomitant substance disorders and severe, chronic psychiatric disorders. The breadth of this problem has been documented by numerous studies measuring the prevalence of substance abuse and substance dependence among chronically mentally ill patients. These studies have indicated a rate of substance abuse—variously defined and measured—of between 32 and 85 percent and prevalence of substance dependence—again variously defined and measured—of between 15 and 40 percent (Pepper, Kirshner, and Ryglewicz, 1981; Schwartz and Goldfinger, 1981; Alterman, 1985; Safer, 1987; Caton, Gralnick, Bender, and Simon, 1989; Drake, Osher, and Wallach, 1989). Similarly, Epidemiologic Catchment Area (ECA) studies have demonstrated a markedly increased prevalence of severe psychiatric disorders, such as schizophrenia and bipolar disorder, among patients with substance dependence diagnoses (Regier and others, 1990).

Such large numbers of dual diagnosis patients have clearly created significant difficulties not only for individual clinicians and programs but also for entire systems of care—both for the addiction system and for the mental health system. Bachrach (1986–1987) has written that these patients are frequently "system misfits"; they do not readily conform to established expectations within each system for obtaining access to care. Addiction programs and addiction clinicians are often ill equipped to deal with addicted patients who present with psychotic symptoms or who require prescription of psychotropic medication, and mental health programs are often similarly ill equipped to treat patients who require an abstinent environment or an intensive addiction recovery support system in which to address substance abuse or dependence. Development of integrated or hybrid programs has been proposed as a solution to this dilemma (Ridgely, Osher, and Talbott, 1987; Osher and Kofoed, 1989; Sciacca, 1987), but even where such programs exist, they cannot adequately respond to either the diversity of dual diagnosis patients or to the sheer numbers of them within any given care system.

The literature on treatment of dual diagnosis patients has described specific clinical techniques (Kofoed, Kania, Walsh, and Atkinson, 1986; Evans and Sullivan, 1990; Osher and Kofoed, 1989) and individual hybrid treatment programs (Ridgely, Osher, and Talbott, 1987; Minkoff, 1989), but with only rare exceptions (Drake and others, 1991), it has not addressed the more complex problem of how to design a comprehensive care *system* to meet the needs of the dual diagnosis population as a whole. The purpose of this chapter is (1) to define specific issues that must be addressed in a comprehensive care system, (2) to describe an integrated theoretical framework for understanding dual diagnosis, and (3) to use this framework to develop a model system of care.

Issues in Designing an Integrated System

The following sections explore some of the key issues to be considered when trying to design an integrated system.

Addiction System Versus Mental Health System. As noted previously, dual diagnosis patients appear with significant frequency in both systems. Consequently, a comprehensive care network for dual diagnosis patients must incorporate and integrate elements of both systems. In a review of selected treatment programs for dual diagnosis patients nationwide, Ridgely, Osher, and Talbott (1987, p. 11) observe that "the fields of mental health and substance abuse have different foci, different philosophies, and a history of contentious behavior toward one another." These philosophical differences include conflicts concerning the use of medication, the quasi-religious nature of twelve-step programs, the predominant role of addiction counselors (as opposed to psychiatrists, psychologists, and social workers) in many addiction programs, the issue of which diagnosis should be primary, and so on. In addition, these philosophical differences are reinforced, in most states, by structural separation of addiction services and mental health services into distinct departments with separate and often competing hierarchies, funding mechanisms, methods for delivering care, patterns of regionalization of services, and organizational cultures (Ridgely, Goldman, and Willenbring, 1990). Separation of administrative authority for mental health and substance abuse services exists in twenty-one of fifty-five states and territories (Ridgely, Goldman, and Willenbring, 1990). This separation is reinforced by the division of the Alcohol, Drug Abuse, and Mental Health Administration (ADAMHA) into three separate institutions (the National Institute of Mental Health [NIMH], the National Institute on Alcohol Abuse and Alcoholism [NIAAA], and the National Institute on Drug Abuse [NIDA]) at the federal level (Ridgely, Goldman, and Willenbring, 1990).

As a result, any workable plan for providing comprehensive services to dual diagnosis patients must either completely reorganize the structure of state government or develop an integrated philosophical perspective that permits each system or department to define a meaningful role in addressing the problem and to identify *focused* areas of intersystem collaboration (Illinois Department of Mental Health and Developmental Disabilities, 1990).

Integrated Treatment Versus Parallel or Sequential Treatment. Any comprehensive care system for dual diagnosis patients must balance reliance on hybrid programs that provide simultaneous addiction and psychiatric treatment (integrated treatment) with utilization of diverse generic program elements that provide individual episodes of psychiatric or addiction treatment to dual diagnosis patients (parallel or sequential treatment). Later in this volume, Kline and colleagues compare the benefits of integrated treatment and parallel treatment in a dually diagnosed homeless mentally ill population. Potential benefits of hybrid treatment include the opportunity to provide simultaneous treatment under one supervisory umbrella, with a unified case management perspective, by dually trained clinicians, in a setting specifically designed to accommodate *both* disorders. A significant problem with this model, however, is the difficulty of developing sufficient numbers and varieties of hybrid programs to accommodate both the numbers of dual diagnosis patients and the variations in their diagnoses, levels of acuity, levels of disability, and degree of motivation.

Parallel treatment, by contrast, allows for utilization of existing treatment resources (with modification) in both care systems. It can have more flexibility in permitting clients to move through the care systems as they progress and to participate in more "normalizing" types of addiction treatment (such as Alcoholics Anonymous [AA] and Narcotics Anonymous). Many patients, particularly those who are homeless, may find it easier to engage with services that do not address mental illness (Kline, Harris, Bebout, and Drake, 1991); others will engage more readily in services that do not address substance abuse. The major limitation of parallel treatment, however, is the enormous burden placed on case managers—and clients— to maintain continuity through multiple episodes of treatment in diverse programs in distinct systems of care. Suitable programs also need to be located for many clients who do not readily fit into existing program models.

Care Versus Confrontation. Traditionally, the mental health system— in particular, the community support system model (Stroul, 1989)—has organized services according to principles of "case management": providing care and support for individuals with various levels of psychiatric disability. The orientation has been to identify individual limitations and deficits and then assertively provide clients *what they need.* Traditional twelve-step addiction programs, by contrast, emphasize individual responsibility and motivation rather than disability. To achieve sobriety, patients must be confronted—in a caring way—by the negative consequences of their addiction in order to generate motivation for recovery. They must then take responsibility for accepting help. The orientation of twelve-step programs, therefore, is to identify the help that is available and then provide people what they are *willing to ask for.* In the mental health system, if a patient refuses help, the case manager takes responsibility and attempts to minimize the negative consequences to the patient. In the addiction system, if a patient refuses help, the clinician is encouraged to "detach" and to allow the patient to bear the responsibility for the negative consequences of his or her refusal.

Clearly, any system of care for dual diagnosis patients must balance care and support for patients' disabilities with empathic confrontation of patients with responsibility for their own recovery. Further, because dual diagnosis patients vary in their levels of disability and motivation, the care system must offer a range of programs that combine care and detachment in various proportions for different patient populations.

Abstinence-Oriented Versus Abstinence-Mandated Programs. A common controversy in programs for dually diagnosed patients is whether to mandate abstinence as a precondition of participation or to encourage abstinence as a goal. Traditional twelve-step programs of addiction treatment clearly indicate that if abstinence is not mandated, the treatment program loses both its credibility and its effectiveness. In contrast, numerous authors (Kofoed, Kania, Walsh, and Atkinson, 1986; Sciacca, 1987; Osher and Kofoed, 1989) have emphasized that, for the dually diagnosed patient, requiring abstinence at the outset discourages or prevents engagement in treatment. Consequently, many hybrid dual diagnosis programs define abstinence as a *goal* and encourage patients to make incremental steps toward that goal through gradual reduction in the amount and frequency of substance use. Such programs may be unable, however, to provide for clients who require a completely abstinent environment in order to initiate or maintain sobriety.

A comprehensive care system for dual diagnosis patients, therefore, may require a *combination* of abstinence-mandated and abstinence-oriented programs, with clear guidelines defining the respective roles of each.

Deinstitutionalization Versus Recovery and Rehabilitation. One issue that faces any care system for the chronically mentally ill is the system's broad definition of its overall mission and philosophy. For several decades, the treatment of the chronically mentally ill has been dominated by the *deinstitutionalization ideology* (Minkoff, 1987). This defines "good care" as care outside of state institutions in community settings, in which the goal is always to encourage the client to utilize the "least-restrictive" and least-intensive alternative, and in which success is measured by reduction in state hospital census and admissions.

Addiction treatment, by contrast, has, in the twelve-step model, been dominated by a philosophy of *recovery,* in which neither locus of care nor short-term morbidity is as significant as the long-term outcome goals of persistent sobriety and growing serenity, self-acceptance, and inner peace. In the recovery model, patients are often encouraged to ask for *more* help in the short run—in more intensive and restrictive settings (inpatient rehabilitation programs, halfway houses, therapeutic communities)—to bring about a more successful long-term outcome.

In recent years, the recovery and rehabilitation ideology has begun to supplant the deinstitutionalization ideology in the treatment of the chronically mentally ill (Harding and others, 1987; Minkoff, 1987), and the role of the patient in taking responsibility for long-term recovery from psychosis has been clarified (Strauss and others, 1987). Thus for the chronically mentally ill (and by extension for the dually diagnosed population), locus of care is becoming less important than maximizing long-term recovery. This implies that extended public hospitalization for dually diagnosed patients may sometimes be appropriate (Group for the Advancement of Psychiatry, 1982). It also means that in some situations, progression to a less restrictive alternative may be made conditional on a patient's taking responsibility for "working a program of recovery" for *both* illnesses.

In designing a system of care for dual diagnosis patients, therefore, the goal of maximizing recovery must be primary but also must be integrated with the goal of minimizing reliance on restrictive institutions. It cannot be expected or assumed, however, that pushing clients into less restrictive settings with more freedom will always enhance the recovery process.

The purpose of this chapter is to describe a comprehensive, continuous, and integrated system of care for dual diagnosis patients that addresses the five issues discussed earlier. To design this system, we need to integrate the simultaneous treatment of mental illness and addiction within a unified conceptual framework.

Integrated Conceptual Framework for Dual Diagnosis

Minkoff (1989) has described an integrated conceptual framework for the treatment of dual diagnosis of serious mental illness and substance dependence in a general hospital inpatient unit. The elements of this conceptual framework are as follows:

1. Chronic psychotic disorders and substance dependence are both viewed as examples of chronic mental illness, with many common characteristics (biological etiology, hereditability, chronicity, incurability, treatability, potential for relapse and deterioration, denial, and associated shame and guilt), despite distinctive differences in symptomatology.

2. Each illness can fit into a disease-and-recovery model for assessment and treatment, where the goal of treatment is to stabilize acute symptoms and then *engage the person* who has the disease to participate in a long-term program of maintenance, rehabilitation, and recovery.

3. Regardless of order of onset, each illness is considered *primary*. Further, although each illness can exacerbate the symptoms of and interfere with the treatment of the other, the severity and level of disability associated with each illness is regarded as essentially *independent* of the severity and level of disability associated with the other. Consequently, patients who have dual diagnoses must receive specific and concurrent treatments for *both* primary diagnoses. For mental illness, this treatment generally involves maintenance medication and rehabilitation programming; for addiction, this treatment involves detoxification, stabilization within a support system such as AA, and participation in a recovery program (for example, twelve steps, residential therapeutic community).

4. Both illnesses can be regarded as having *parallel* phases of treatment and recovery. According to Minkoff (1989), those phases include acute stabilization, engagement in treatment, prolonged stabilization and maintenance, and rehabilitation and recovery. Osher and Kofoed (1989) have further subdivided the engagement phase into engagement, persuasion, and active treatment; prolonged stabilization is the intended outcome of active treatment.

5. Although, in dual diagnosis patients, progress in recovery for each diagnosis is *affected* by progress in recovery for the other, the recovery processes commonly proceed independently. In particular, progress in recovery may depend on patient motivation, and patient motivation for treatment of each illness may vary. Thus patients may be engaged in active treatment to maintain stabilization of psychosis, while still refusing treatment for stabilization of substance abuse. Alternatively, patients may be actively sober in AA yet deny the need for psychotropic medication for mental illness (Minkoff, 1989).

This conceptual framework has the following implications for designing a dual diagnosis system of care:

Each care system must include program elements that meet the needs of patients in *each phase of recovery for each illness*. Thus some programs may provide active treatment for one illness and maintenance for the other. There must, for example, be programs for acute detoxification of stable mentally ill individuals, as well as programs for patients who require simultaneous detoxification and stabilization of psychosis; programs for beginning the process of engagement and persuasion to involve stable mentally ill patients in substance abuse treatment, and programs for stable mentally ill patients who want and need active abstinence-mandated addiction treatment; and so on. Each care system must include program elements that address various levels of *severity* and *disability* in each illness in each phase of recovery. For example, there may be a range of community residence programs that includes a residence appropriate for severely disabled mentally ill people with substance problems that are amenable to outpatient treatment, a residence appropriate for highly functioning mentally ill individuals who are severely addicted and need an abstinent environment to maintain sobriety, and a residence for people who are severely ill with both illnesses.

Each system of care must include program elements suitable for clients who have various levels of *motivation* for assuming responsibility for their recovery. The system must provide adequate levels of care for those who are disabled but unmotivated, while creating systemwide incentives for clients to progress to programs that are more desirable but also more demanding.

Some dual diagnosis programs will ideally be extensions of existing generic programs within either the addiction or mental health system into which dual diagnosis patients are integrated. Others will be specific hybrid programs that serve *only* dually diagnosed patients. The illness being treated most actively; the phase of treatment; and the patient's level of severity, disability, and motivation will determine within which system a program is best located and whether the program should be generic or specific.

Development of a Model System of Care

Bachrach (1986) has identified continuity and comprehensiveness as key elements in the design of a model system of care. I will discuss each element separately.

Continuity. Within any comprehensive array of services, the care system needs to provide for continuity of treatment between programs, as well as continuity over time. This is a particular problem for dual diagnosis patients, who often experience "ping-pong treatment" (Ridgely, Goldman, and Willenbring, 1990) as they bounce back and forth between two distinct care systems. Although involvement of patients in ongoing hybrid programs facilitates continuity of care, most patients will still need to be involved with multiple programs in different phases of treatment throughout their long-term course. Consequently, development of an integrated dual diagnosis case management program is a necessary ingredient in creating a dual diagnosis care system.

Ideally, dual diagnosis case management involves both the addiction system and the mental health system. Although dual diagnosis case management programs have been created entirely within the mental health system utilizing teams of dually trained clinicians (Harris and Bergman, 1987), the most recent models have been developed through statewide collaborations between mental health and substance abuse authorities (Drake, Teague, and Warren, 1990; Illinois Department of Mental Health and Developmental Disabilities, 1990). In both New Hampshire and Illinois, in fact, the implementation of a collaborative dual diagnosis case management program has been the necessary first step in pulling together diverse program components to provide individual patients with a beginning comprehensive system of care.

Comprehensiveness. As previously discussed, a comprehensive care system for dual diagnosis patients will include programs within both the addiction system and the mental health system, as well as some collaborative programs. Integrated treatment programs will be one type of program element within a broad parallel treatment model that incorporates a range of hybrid and generic programs. Programs will be designed to focus on different phases of treatment and different levels of motivation, severity, and disability related to each illness and will include both abstinence-oriented and abstinence-mandated programs. Programs will be defined by the level of care and support provided, and the level of patient responsibility expected, for treatment of each illness.

One principle I have used in developing this model is to build on existing systems and programs wherever possible and to minimize the extent to which additional specialized dual diagnosis programs must be developed. This approach is not only less costly, but it reflects the reality that dual diagnosis is so prevalent that it must be addressed (to some extent) as part of *routine* treatment in either care system.

Unfortunately, in some states existing care systems for single diagnosis patients are sadly deficient. In such states, more creative solutions for dual diagnosis patients will be necessary. For example, in a state that has little public funding available for alcohol and drug treatment, the mental health system may have to take a leadership role in developing generic addiction detoxification or rehabilitation services as a resource for dually diagnosed clients.

Programs for Each Phase of Treatment

I will now describe the specific programs in this model for each phase of treatment of each illness.

Acute Stabilization. For dual diagnosis patients, acute stabilization of psychiatric symptoms generally occurs within the mental health system, usually in an acute psychiatric inpatient unit. Patients with less severe symptoms may be treated in outpatient or day hospital settings, whereas patients with the most severe disturbances will require access to a locked facility. Ries (1990) has observed that severe behavioral symptoms (psychosis, violence, suicidality) may require acute psychiatric inpatient treatment, even when such symptoms are solely related to substance abuse. To treat patients with coexisting substance disorders, the traditional acute psychiatric unit needs to develop the following capabilities: (1) capacity to provide detoxification for substance-dependent patients, (2) protocols to identify substance abuse and dependence disorders, (3) capacity to initiate education and engagement regarding substance use, and (4) referral linkages to programs that can continue the process of engagement for both substance disorders and psychiatric disorders.

Acute stabilization of addiction symptoms within the addiction system usually occurs in a detoxification program. Less severely ill addiction patients can discontinue use without detoxification or receive detoxification on an outpatient basis: access to a methadone maintenance program may provide outpatient acute stabilization for narcotic addicts. More severely substance-dependent individuals who are endangering themselves or others and who are unable to accept help yet do not have acute psychiatric symptoms may require involuntary detoxification.

With regard to dual diagnosis patients, the generic detoxification programs listed earlier are potentially appropriate for individuals with (1) stable psychotic mental illness without severe residual symptoms, (2) personality disorders without severe behavioral disturbance, or (3) a range of anxiety, depressive, and post-traumatic stress disorders. To accommodate such patients, the following capacities can be developed: (1) ability to provide medication other than for detoxification (stable regimen only) and to support its continued use if indicated, (2) protocols for assessment of coexisting psychiatric disorder and for ensuring sufficient psychiatric stability to permit admission, (3) availability of psychiatric consultation for difficult cases, and (4) referral linkage to both acute and maintenance psychiatric programs and to engagement programs for substance dependence.

In some areas, specialized detoxification programs have been developed collaboratively to address the needs of patients who have behavioral disturbances *while intoxicated* that are too severe for a standard detoxification program but that resolve without other specific intervention (for example, personality-disordered alcoholics who are suicidal when drunk) and therefore do not require psychiatric hospitalization.

Engagement, Education, and Persuasion. For most dual diagnosis patients, engagement in treatment for major mental illness generally occurs within the mental health system, most commonly in an inpatient unit following acute stabilization. The most severely psychotic patients may require involuntary treatment and involuntary medication and occasionally prolonged hospitalization in a public mental hospital. By contrast, many patients, particularly homeless mentally ill individuals, are engaged through community-based intensive care management and outreach programs (Harris and Bergman, 1987; Kline, Harris, Bebout, and Drake, 1991). As noted earlier, such programs must also have the capacity to initiate education and engagement regarding coexisting substance disorders. In addition, they should either provide or have referral linkages to programs that provide ongoing stabilization for mental illness and continuing engagement and persuasion efforts regarding substance abuse (see the following discussion).

For most addiction patients, engagement in treatment for substance abuse in the addiction system occurs during the "rehabilitation" phase of inpatient addiction treatment. With the advent of managed care, many programs are also developing intensive day and evening treatment models (Batten and others, 1989). Such programs mandate abstinence as a condition of participation and can be suitable for *motivated* dual diagnosis patients who have (1) stable psychotic mental illness without severe residual symptoms, (2) personality disorders without severe behavioral disturbance, or (3) a range of coexisting anxiety, depressive, and post-traumatic stress disorders. To accommodate such patients, the capacities listed earlier for detoxification programs must be available, as well as referrals to long-term addiction support programs such as outpatient AA and residential settings.

Integrated addiction and psychiatric units, such as that described by Minkoff (1989), can be ideal settings to initiate engagement in treatment for both illnesses simultaneously, particularly for patients whose psychiatric symptoms are not completely stabilized or are more severe at baseline. Such a program can also provide more in-depth assessment of difficult "dual diagnostic dilemmas." In systems where such an integrated program is not available, simultaneous parallel treatment in neighboring collaborative units can sometimes work nearly as well. Less beneficial is sequential treatment in noncollaborative programs (Ries, 1990; Ridgely, Goldman, and Willenbring, 1990).

Engagement in treatment for substance *abuse* (as distinct from dependence) for mentally ill patients—and for all substance disorders for more severely disabled mentally ill patients—generally begins in the setting in which the patient is receiving treatment for ongoing stabilization of the mental illness.

Ongoing Stabilization and Rehabilitation Within the mental health system, ongoing stabilization, treatment, and rehabilitation for dually diagnosed patients occur in a range of outpatient, day treatment, and residential settings, depending on the level of severity of patients' disabilities and to a lesser extent on their willingness to comply with treatment requirements. The most severely ill and least motivated require long-term residential treatment and self-contained day programming in public mental hospitals; those with illnesses of moderate severity live in supervised residences or in the care of family members and participate in various types of day programming; and those with the least-severe illnesses may live independently and participate in standard outpatient treatment. Homeless patients may be engaged in ongoing case management and day programming even prior to receiving housing (Harris and Bergman, 1987).

Dual diagnosis patients engaged in mental health treatment in these settings are frequently unwilling either to recognize or to seek treatment for their coexisting substance disorders. Consequently, each of these settings needs to develop integrated or hybrid program models that address substance abuse and substance dependence within the setting itself.

Several such models are described in the literature (Osher and Kofoed, 1989; Sciacca, 1987) and in later chapters in this volume. Common characteristics of these programs in the *outpatient* setting are as follows:

1. Abstinence is a goal, not a requirement.
2. Patients with substance abuse and substance dependence are treated together.

3. Group models, with either staff or peer leaders, are fundamental.
4. Patients progress from (a) low-level education or "persuasion" groups, in which patients have high denial and low motivation, to (b) "active treatment" groups, in which they are more motivated to consider abstinence and are willing to accept more confrontation, to (c) abstinence support groups, in which they have mostly committed to abstinence and help each other learn new skills to attain or maintain sobriety (Osher and Kofoed, 1989).
5. Involvement of available family members is recommended.

Residential programming has similar goals and generally can incorporate a variety of residential models:

1. Integrating dual diagnosis patients into a generic mental health residence and providing substance abuse treatment as part of a day program
2. Creating a dual diagnosis residence with abstinence as a goal and with on-site dual diagnosis groups
3. Developing a sober residence for *motivated* patients who require residential support, in which abstinence is mandated, or at least expected, and in which abstinence-support programming is built in

Note that these distinctions can even be created within subdivisions of a state hospital.

Regardless of the type of substance programming offered, each program must define the level of substance-related problem behavior that cannot be tolerated within the program (for example, obvious intoxication, belligerence, selling or using drugs on premises, and so on) and develop a clear set of policies that determine the behavioral consequences for violations (Sciacca, 1991). Such policies are not punitive but rather provide necessary protection from drugs and alcohol, safety for other program participants, and leverage to encourage offending patients to accept more intensive substance dependence treatment, perhaps in an inpatient addiction unit. Consequences are only valid if they can be enforced, and provision *must* be made in the care system for patients who are suspended or discharged from day or residential programs due to persistent out-of-control substance involvement. In many systems, this will require making state hospitals available (deinstitutionalization ideology notwithstanding) for severely psychiatrically disabled actively addicted and unmotivated patients who otherwise might become homeless. In some locations, as an alternative, "wet" residential programs have been developed, where almost any amount of substance abuse can be tolerated (Blankertz and White, 1990).

Within the addiction system, extended support to maintain sobriety for severely addicted patients is generally available through a network of halfway houses (three to twelve months), therapeutic communities (twelve to twenty-four months), and sober houses (long-term), all of which are abstinence programs. Such programs are appropriate for motivated dual diagnosis patients who are otherwise capable of independent living, have reasonable social skills, and meet the diagnostic criteria listed earlier. These programs need to provide specialized training to staff in assessment and treatment of psychiatric disorders and permit patients to self-administer stable regimens of nonaddictive medications. Psychiatric consultation is essential and is best provided through linkage with an affiliated mental health provider that assumes concurrent and ongoing responsibility for the psychiatric treatment of these patients. In addition, such programs must provide linkage to ongoing outpatient *addiction* treatment, including individual, group, and family counseling, as well as twelve-step programs.

Traditional twelve-step programs in the addiction system are a valuable component of the ongoing addiction support system for dual diagnosis patients (Kofoed, Kania, Walsh, and Atkinson, 1986), particularly for patients who receive "special preparation" for selecting suitable groups and learning how to use the program properly (Ridgely, Osher, and Talbott, 1987; Minkoff, 1989). Even state hospital patients with severe psychiatric disabilities have been able to use twelve-step program attendance as an adjunctive support in maintaining sobriety.

Finally, collaborative or integrated programs to support ongoing stabilization and recovery can be developed in either system. Residences that provide a therapeutic community environment for treatment of addiction along with an infusion of psychiatric services for treatment of mental illness have emerged in the addiction system (McLaughlin and Pepper, 1991), and traditional psychiatric residences that mandate sobriety with an intense addiction treatment focus have emerged in the mental health system. Often these programs are cofunded or cosponsored by federal, state, or local mental health and addiction treatment authorities. Similarly, twelve-step programs specifically for dual diagnosis patients have emerged under the auspices of AA ("Double Trouble" meetings), and where such meetings do not exist, dual diagnosis peer-support groups using twelve-step principles can be developed in the mental health system.

Conclusion

I have described the dilemmas involved in dual diagnosis treatment and have used a unified conceptual framework to design a model of a comprehensive, continuous, and integrated system of care for dual diagnosis patients. This model can be used by (1) system planners, to identify gaps that can be addressed by new program initiatives or by additional training resources, (2) program managers, to identify the role of each program within the total system and how to improve the program's capacity to treat dual diagnosis patients, and (3) individual case managers, to assess the capacities of their own system in relation to the needs of individual clients.

Although the model contains generic as well as hybrid treatment programs, more successful systems will be characterized by better-developed case management and a greater number and variety of hybrid or integrated programs.

References

Alterman, A. I. "Substance Abuse in Psychiatric Patients." In A. I. Alterman (ed.), *Substance Abuse and Psychopathology*. New York: Plenum, 1985.

Bachrach, L. "The Challenge of Service Planning for Chronic Mental Patients." *Community Mental Health Journal*, 1986, *22*, 170–174.

Bachrach, L. "The Context of Care for the Chronic Mental Patient with Substance Abuse." *Psychiatric Quarterly*, 1986–1987, *58*, 3–14.

Batten, H. L., and others. "Implementation Issues in Addictions Day Treatment." *Hospital and Health Services Administration*, 1989, *34*(3), 427–439.

Blankertz, L., and White, K. K. "Implementation of a Rehabilitation Program for Dually Diagnosed Homeless." *Alcoholism Treatment Quarterly*, 1990, *7*, 149–164.

Caton, C.L.M., Gralnick, A., Bender, S., and Simon, R. "Young Chronic Patients and Substance Abuse." *Hospital and Community Psychiatry*, 1989, *40*(ed10), 1037–1040.

Drake, R. E., Osher, F. C., and Wallach, M. A. "Alcohol Use and Abuse in Schizophrenia: A Prospective Community Study." *Journal of Nervous and Mental Disease*, 1989, *177*, 408–414.

Drake, R. E., Teague, G. B., and Warren, S. R. "New Hampshire's Program for People Dually Diagnosed with Severe Mental Illness and Substance Use Disorders." *Addiction and Recovery*, 1990, *10*, 35–39.

Drake, R. E., and others. "New Hampshire's Specialized Services for the Dually Diagnosed." In K. Minkoff and R.E. Drake (eds.), *Dual Diagnosis of Major Mental Illness and Substance Disorder*. New Directions for Mental Health Services, no. 50. San Francisco: Jossey-Bass, 1991.

Evans, K., and Sullivan, J. M. *Dual Diagnosis: Counseling the Mentally Ill Substance Abuser*. New York: Guilford Press, 1990.

Group for the Advancement of Psychiatry. *The Positive Aspects of Long-Term Hospitalization in the Public Sector for Chronic Psychiatric Patients*. Report no. 10. New York: Mental Health Materials Center, 1982.

Harding, C. M., and others. "The Vermont Longitudinal Study of Persons with Severe Mental Illness, II: Long-Term Outcome of Subjects Who Retrospectively Met DSM-III Criteria for Schizophrenia." *American Journal of Psychiatry*, 1987, *144*, 727–735.

Harris, M., and Bergman, H. "Case Management with the Chronically Mentally Ill: A Clinical Perspective." *American Journal of Orthopsychiatry*, 1987, *57*(ed2), 296–302.

Illinois Department of Mental Health and Developmental Disabilities. *Task Force Report for the Mentally Ill Substance Abuser*. Springfield: Illinois Department of Mental Health and Developmental Disabilities, 1990.

Kline, J., Harris M., Bebout, R. R., and Drake, R. E. "Contrasting Integrated and Linkage Models of Treatment for Homeless, Dually Diagnosed Adults." In K. Minkoff and R. E. Drake (eds.), *Dual Diagnosis of Major Mental Illness and Substance Disorder*. New Directions for Mental Health Services, no. 50. San Francisco: Jossey-Bass, 1991.

Kofoed, L., Kania, J., Walsh, T., and Atkinson, R. "Outpatient Treatment of Patients with Substance Abuse and Coexisting Psychiatric Disorders." *American Journal of Psychiatry*, 1986, *143*, 867–872.

McLaughlin, P., and Pepper, B. "Modifying the Therapeutic Community for the Mentally Ill Substance Abuser." In K. Minkoff and R. E. Drake (eds.), *Dual Diagnosis of Major Mental Illness and Substance Disorder*. New Directions for Mental Health Services, no. 50. San Francisco: Jossey-Bass, 1991.

Minkoff, K. "Beyond Deinstitutionalization: A New Ideology for the Postinstitutional Era." *Hospital and Community Psychiatry,* 1987, *38,* 945–950.

Minkoff, K. "An Integrated Treatment Model for Dual Diagnosis of Psychosis and Addiction." *Hospital and Community Psychiatry,* 1989, *40*(ed10), 1031–1036.

Osher, F. C., and Kofoed, L. L. "Treatment of Patients with Psychiatric and Psychoactive Substance Abuse Disorders." *Hospital and Community Psychiatry,* 1989, *40,* 1025–1030.

Pepper, B., Kirshner, M. C., and Ryglewicz, H. "The Young Adult Chronic Patient: Overview of a Population." *Hospital and Community Psychiatry,* 1981, *32,* 463–469.

Regier, D. A., and others. "Comorbidity of Mental Disorders with Alcohol and Other Drug Abuse." Results from the Epidemiologic Catchment Area (ECA) Study. *Journal of the American Medical Association,* 1990, *264*(ed19), 2511–2518.

Ridgely, M. S., Goldman, H. H., and Willenbring, M. "Barriers to the Care of Persons with Dual Diagnoses: Organizational and Financing Issues." *Schizophrenia Bulletin,* 1990, *16*(ed1), 123–132.

Ridgely, M. S., Osher, F. C., and Talbott, J. A. *Chronic Mentally Ill Young Adults with Substance Abuse Problems: Treatment and Training Issues.* Baltimore: Mental Health Policy Studies, School of Medicine, University of Maryland, 1987.

Ries, R. "Acute, Subacute, and Maintenance Treatment Phases for Dual Diagnosis Patients with the Public Mental Health Center." Unpublished manuscript, Department of Psychiatry, University of Washington, 1990.

Safer, D. J. "Substance Abuse by Young Adult Chronic Patients." *Hospital and Community Psychiatry,* 1987, *38,* 511–514.

Schwartz, S. R., and Goldfinger, S. M. "The New Chronic Patient: Clinical Characteristics of an Emerging Subgroup." *Hospital and Community Psychiatry,* 1981, *32,* 470–474.

Sciacca, K. "New Initiatives in the Treatment of the Chronic Patient with Alcohol/Substance Use Problems." *TIE Lines,* 1987, *4*(ed3), 5–6.

Sciacca, K. "An Integrated Treatment Approach for Severly Mentally Ill Individuals with Substance Disorders." In K. Minkoff and R. E. Drake (eds.), *Dual Diagnosis of Major Mental Illness and Substance Disorder.* New Directions for Mental Health Services, no. 50. San Francisco: Jossey-Bass, 1991.

Strauss, J. S., and others. "The Role of the Patient in Recovery from Psychosis." In J. S. Strauss, W. Boker, and H. D. Brenner (eds.), *Psychosocial Treatment of Schizophrenia.* Toronto: Huber, 1987.

Stroul, B. A. "Community Support Systems for Persons with Long-Term Mental Illness: A Conceptual Framework." *Psychosocial Rehabilitation Journal,* 1989, *12,* 9–26.

KENNETH MINKOFF *is medical director of Choate Integrated Behavioral Care in Woburn, Massachusetts, and assistant clinical professor of psychiatry at Harvard Medical School.*

3

This chapter provides guidelines, illustrated with case examples, for combining individual and family treatment of outpatients vulnerable to psychosis.

Combining Individual and Family Treatment: Guidelines for the Therapist

Nancy C. Atwood

Treating outpatients who are vulnerable to psychosis is a test of the therapist's skill and commitment. Involving the families of patients adds to the complexity of treatment. However, it also increases its potential for successful outcome, because what happens with patients and how well they do is affected by how the patient and the family interact.

When psychosis-prone patients live with their relatives, it is almost inevitable that families will come to the attention of the therapist, whether the therapist seeks them out or not. Patients talk about their families, and it inevitably becomes clear that their families are very important in their lives. In turn, families often contact the therapist to talk about the patient and to express their concerns.

Therapists can choose to respond either passively or actively to the family's influence in the patient's life. Taking a proactive rather than a reactive position gives the therapist a chance to have a direct impact on the environment in which the patient lives and on how the patient deals with that environment.

This chapter recommends that the therapist take an active stance vis-à-vis families, particularly when the patient is living at home with parents or a spouse. It provides guidelines and case examples to show how the therapist can take the initiative to involve families in the treatment process, while still preserving the primary focus on individual therapy and the therapist-patient relationship. The guidelines are based on the author's experience in outpatient settings and on clinical literature about integrative approaches to the treatment of schizophrenia and major affective disorders (Anderson, Reiss, and Hogarty, 1986; Bernheim

NEW DIRECTIONS FOR MENTAL HEALTH SERVICES, no. 91, Fall 2001   © John Wiley & Sons, Inc.

and Lehman, 1985; Davenport and Adland, 1985; De Nour, 1980; Jamison, 1987; Roberts, 1984). This work is an elaboration and expansion of a previously published article on integrating individual and family treatment for outpatients vulnerable to psychosis (Atwood, 1990).

The case examples that follow, particularly those that illustrate what *not* to do, imply that the treatment of psychotic patients is fraught with hazard. Indeed, the work sometimes takes on a "life-and-death" quality that reflects the often-dominating role of major mental illness in the lives of patients and families. This chapter does not minimize that sense of risk but rather suggests principles and techniques that therapists can use in attempting to make the benefits of treatment outweigh the risks.

Principles of Treatment

The principles proposed here are not intended to be rigid prescriptions for care, but rather guidelines for the clinician to keep in mind in approaching the problems of combining individual and family treatment. Though in some instances clinical judgment may prompt the clinician to deviate from these principles, for the great majority of patients they provide a sound basis for thinking about combined treatment.

1. *Attend to information about the patient that the family provides, and instead of ignoring it or dismissing it as biased, assume that it may well be accurate.* The heart of psychotherapy is the interchange between patient and therapist. Therapists base their assessment of patients primarily on face-to-face interactions and not on what other people—including relatives—tell them. However, treating individuals who are vulnerable to psychosis sometimes requires turning to others for information. Psychosis often inhibits and distorts communication to such an extent that to ignore what relatives say is to keep out data that may be essential for understanding the patient, managing the case, and protecting the patient from harm (Intagliata, Wilner, and Egri, 1986).

Although family members can have distorted perspectives and complex motives in describing patient behavior, family reporting regarding psychotic symptoms and behaviors is more likely than not to be reasonably accurate. In making judgments about information from family members—information that relates to the patient's psychosis—the clinician should operate on the presumption that the family member is reporting accurately. The following case is an extreme illustration of this principle. Forced to make a choice between information from a direct encounter with a patient and information from a spouse, the clinician chose to dismiss the family information, and a suicide occurred that might otherwise have been prevented.

> A senior psychiatrist began treatment on an emergency basis of a thirty-one-year-old medical resident who worked at the same hospital as he did. The precipitant for the visits was that the patient's wife had suddenly disappeared, taking their two children with her. The patient was distraught but denied suicidality or any

history of homicidality, and the clinician detected no signs of psychosis. The patient was able to function at work and was taking steps to locate his wife.

After scheduling an appointment to see his patient again in five days, the psychiatrist departed for a professional conference. When he returned, he received a call from his patient's wife, who had finally returned with their children. Crying hysterically over the phone, she described violence at home occurring after she told her husband that she had seen a lawyer about a divorce. Her husband, she said, tried to strangle her and then left the house in the middle of the night. She had difficulty describing his state in detail, but she was convinced that he "was no longer himself." "He seemed to be out of his mind," she said. "I've never seen him act so strange."

When the wife came to the psychiatrist's office the next morning, he saw several bruises on her neck. She said that her husband had been talking about suicide and might have gone to their summer hunting lodge in the northern part of the state. She asked the psychiatrist to contact the police, expressing great concern for her husband's safety.

In evaluating the situation, the clinician determined that the wife was "overreacting." He felt confident in his observation that the patient was not psychotic and not suicidal, and he assumed that the main danger was domestic violence because of the patient's rage about the separation. He therefore warned her against letting her husband back in the house if he should return and strongly reassured her that he had assessed the patient and that he was not a suicidal risk. Two days later, the body of the young physician was found lying on the floor of their summer cottage, shot through the head.

In this case, the psychiatrist had the opportunity to learn enough about his patient from a family member to justify emergency action, but he failed to appreciate its urgency. Had he explored the wife's concerns in greater depth, he might have been more willing to consider the possibility of acute psychosis and severe suicidal risk.

In some instances, family members provide information that is crucial to the therapeutic process. The case report that follows shows how timely information from a relative can be the missing piece that explains otherwise inexplicable behavior.

A forty-five-year-old divorced factory worker had lost custody of her children after her third manic episode. Her married, childless sister, a teacher, was guardian for the woman's three teenage children. The woman lived alone but visited her children regularly.

At the outset of individual treatment with a psychiatric resident, the woman—then stabilized—suggested inviting her sister to a therapy session. During this meeting the patient treated her sister deferentially, but in subsequent individual sessions deference turned to resentment and then to anger. As she became hypomanic, she vilified her sister, describing her as traitorous for taking her children away and incompetent as a surrogate parent.

Around this time, the therapist received a call from the sister. She told the therapist that she had something important to tell him that might shed light on her sister's change in attitude. About a month before, when the patient was stable, her sister suggested that they go together to a school science fair at which one of the children had an exhibit. When they got there and her son saw them, he enthusiastically told his aunt about his project but ignored his mother. Ever since, the caller said, her sister had been getting more and more hostile.

The therapist had heard nothing about this incident from the patient. After adjusting his patient's medication and scheduling extra meetings, he gently encouraged her to talk about her relationship with her son, eventually eliciting a tearful account of the incident. With continued support from her therapist, she gradually recompensated and a manic episode was averted.

In this example, the therapist took a telephone call from a relative and exercised judgment about how to handle the information provided. Some therapists believe that it is a violation of patient confidentiality to receive telephone calls from family members. In fact, listening by itself does not violate confidentiality, which is violated only if the therapist then discloses material from therapy sessions without prior permission from the patient.

2. *Wherever possible, give decision-making authority to the patient. Do not collude with the family to treat the patient as incompetent.* Professionals, like the general public, are understandably skeptical about the competence of people who are vulnerable to psychosis, even when they are free of psychotic symptoms. Clinicians must nevertheless guard against this bias and see the patient phenomenologically and unlabeled, as he or she actually is at any point in time. When they do this, clinicians are likely to allow self-determination to a patient who is not incapacitated by psychosis. A therapist who has this respectful attitude toward the patient also models behavior based on this attitude for the family, thereby increasing the likelihood that the family will treat the patient respectfully as well.

In the following case illustration, a well-intentioned but misguided therapist indirectly interfered with the self-determination of a schizophrenic woman out of concern for her capacity to handle a difficult situation. Fortunately, another therapist perceived the woman's capabilities correctly and encouraged her to take an action that she was competent to perform.

A therapist was treating Mr. A., a thirty-five-year-old lab technician, for dysthymia. His wife, who was in separate individual treatment with another therapist, had been diagnosed as schizophrenic during the second year of their marriage. Although deeply troubled by her illness, Mr. A. described his wife as intelligent and often affectionate and had remained loyal to her through the course of her several hospitalizations.

Mrs. A. had had a thought disorder most of the time since the birth of a son early in their marriage. When the couple was no longer able to care for the child, they acquiesced to his being placed in foster care. Every week, they visited the little boy and played with him at the home of his foster parents.

Eventually, the foster family wanted to adopt the child. Mr. A. told his therapist that he knew that his wife and he were not capable of raising their son and that the foster parents were good people who loved him. He agreed to have the foster family become permanent parents in an open adoption.

Meanwhile, Mrs. A.'s therapist was working with her to help her accept the necessity of adoption for her son. Although Mrs. A. angrily objected at times, she eventually assented and a court date was set to formalize the adoption. Mr. A. told his therapist that he did not want his wife to appear in court. He was afraid that she might balk at the last minute, object to the adoption, and become overtly psychotic in front of the judge.

His therapist agreed. He judged that having Mrs. A. in the courtroom was too risky and might subject his wife to more stress than she could handle. He felt it would be preferable to have Mrs. A. sign the adoption papers outside of the courtroom. Mr. A.'s therapist called the couple's lawyer to express this preference and cautioned the lawyer against allowing Mrs. A. to testify.

However, Mrs. A. felt differently, and her therapist backed her up. She felt strongly that it was *her* child whose disposition was at issue and that she had a right to be in court to relinquish him herself. Mrs. A. and her therapist took a strong stand and actively registered their disagreement with the lawyer. As a result, her wish was respected, and she participated appropriately in the courtroom process. She told the judge in a coherent way why she was willing to give her child up for adoption and drew considerable comfort and satisfaction from the experience.

3. *Involve the family in the treatment on a regular basis.* Patients vulnerable to psychosis are often completely dependent on their families for the basic necessities of life. Because of this, their everyday well-being is crucially affected by what happens within the family. Under these circumstances, a clinician has no other choice but to involve the family in the treatment on a regular basis because the family, not the patient, determines the environment in which the patient lives. In the following case, a clinician was able to accept the reality of the patient's dependency and the family's authority while still attending to the individual needs of the patient.

A clinician received a call about a prospective forty-year-old female patient. The caller was the older married sister of the prospective patient and was the woman's guardian. The caller said that her younger sister, who was diagnosed as schizophrenic, needed a new home. Her younger sister had always lived with their parents, had never been normal, and had taken antipsychotic medication for several years. Their father had died recently, and their elderly mother had suffered a stroke.

Before his death, their father had arranged for guardianship and a trust fund for his daughter. Now that the father was dead, the older sister was ready to assume responsibility. Their mother was no longer able to cope with her daughter, who had temper tantrums and had never helped at home. Furthermore, the caller's husband was insisting that his sister-in-law get settled into a permanent home lest they themselves become her caretakers when the mother died.

The caller said that this was her second attempt to get help for her sister. For several weeks, she had driven her sister to a mental health clinic for appointments that had not led anywhere. At the clinic, the counselor met alone with her sister and had refused to tell the older sister anything about the meeting or about finding a new place for her sister to live. Out of frustration, the older sister had decided not to take her sister back to that clinic and was calling to see if another kind of help was available.

The clinician agreed to see the patient and found her docilely accepting of her sister's management of her case. The clinician began weekly meetings with the patient, held joint meetings with the patient and her sister, and also met with the older sister and her husband. The clinician made a home visit to the mother, whose fragility and stiffness toward her daughter pointed up the need for an alternative living situation. Based on these observations, the clinician concluded that it was clearly the older sister and not the mother to whom the patient was emotionally attached.

Over the course of several months, the clinician combined supportive counseling and resource referral in an effort to place her patient in a community-based residence and a day activity. Occasionally, the patient, her sister, and the clinician went together to visit a prospective residence, but the right place eluded them. Finally, the patient was accepted at a board-and-care home. She was able to make the transition without significant difficulty and adjusted well to her new surroundings. She attended a social club for the mentally ill and continued treatment with her clinician at the clinic every other week.

4. *Even when the family is resistant or difficult to work with, the clinician should not allow that fact to justify avoiding family involvement.* Working with patients individually is easier than working with families. The problem is that individual treatment by itself is not likely to work if a patient lives at home and is actually or potentially psychotic. Sooner or later, the patient may regress or succumb to psychosis because family life is inherently stressful. If the family has characteristics like the one described in the next case report, the chances are good that the patient will succumb sooner rather than later. Not paradoxically, these characteristics—alcoholism, violence, and a major family secret—are the very ones that might lead a therapist to put off or avoid working with this family.

A therapist began seeing a twenty-three-year-old male storeroom clerk for individual therapy. The patient had two prior psychiatric hospitalizations for major depression with psychotic features and was on probation following an arrest for drunk driving. The patient lived at home with his mother, stepfather, a grandmother, and three siblings. A written record from a previous hospitalization described his family as "chaotic," especially because of his stepfather's alcohol abuse. It also said that the patient had been told that his father was killed in Vietnam, when in reality his father was alive, having abandoned his unmarried mother soon after he was born.

In therapy, the clinician focused the sessions on the patient's adjustment to the new job for which the patient had trained in a vocational adjustment program. The patient took his job very seriously, and the therapist encouraged him to talk about his work. Occasionally, the patient talked about home—about quarrels between his mother and stepfather, insistent requests from his grandmother to do chores, and teasing from his younger sisters about being "wacko."

He spoke of lonely hours upstairs in his room, looking out his window at former neighborhood friends whom he used to hang out with but now avoided. At one point, his therapist proposed inviting his mother in to talk about the home situation. The patient said that was all right but that she worked and could not come in during the day. The therapist dropped the subject.

A few weeks later, the therapist received a call from a hospital emergency room. Her patient, psychotic and angry, had been brought into the emergency room by his mother and the police after a fight with his stepfather. His mother told the emergency room staff that she had known for several weeks that their son often sat in his car after work, drinking beer. He was hospitalized in a psychiatric unit and then spent five months in a day treatment program before returning to a program of vocational training.

This patient's way of dealing with intolerable stress was to withdraw from the family physically and through alcohol. The therapist colluded with that withdrawal by virtually ignoring the family, thereby permitting the buildup of the family tensions that preceded the patient's breakdown.

How might the situation have been handled differently? The therapist could have invited the family for a meeting with her and the patient at the outset of treatment. This meeting would have given all participants—the therapist, the patient, and the family—a chance to observe one another, share information, and form a working relationship. This meeting might have made it clear from the beginning that the therapist, the patient, and the family shared an interest in the patient's recovery and would try to work together. After that, it would have been up to the therapist to push for the convening of such meetings, probably holding them in the evening so both parents could attend.

Involving a family such as this might have been difficult, but not impossible, as they themselves, particularly the parents, were affected by the patient's behavior and undoubtedly had strong feelings about his presence among them. Many families accept a therapist pushing for their involvement once they see that the therapist is genuinely interested in the patient and capable of providing help. Families are likely to appreciate the chance to express themselves about problems that they are having with the patient as long as they see the family meetings as helpful in dealing with those problems. It is only when families perceive that the treatment *adds* to their burden that they balk and refuse to participate (Johnson, 1990; Dearth, Labenski, Mott, and Pellegrini, 1986).

The focus of such meetings should be on what the family and the patient perceive as problematic, particularly as these problems relate to the patient's functioning. For example, in the case just discussed, the therapist might focus a session on what chores the patient is expected to do at home and attempt to arrive at a family consensus, including agreement from the patient, about how to implement that expectation. Later, in individual treatment, the therapist could explore further with the patient his attitude toward those chores and the process of doing them.

Actual and potential alcohol abuse heightens the need for therapist-family interaction, because the abuse generally occurs outside the therapist's awareness and is likely to be denied. By becoming familiar with the daily patterns of life of the patient and the family, the therapist could assess alcohol use and intervene where necessary.

There is still another way to look at a family situation like this. A therapist might hope that the patient will want to move away from home and find an alternative, less "chaotic" environment. Certainly, assessing the likelihood of such a separation and even encouraging it are appropriate, but actually bringing separation about is another matter. For one reason or another, patients and families often need and want to live together. The therapist's role is to accept that reality and work with it, building on whatever strengths the family possesses to help the patient improve and function as adequately as possible (Group for the Advancement of Psychiatry, 1986).

5. *Although family participation in treatment is important, family therapy by itself is not enough to support the patient and manage the treatment. Maintain the primary focus on individual therapy and on the therapist-patient relationship.* Individual treatment is essential for patients who are vulnerable to psychosis. Although other interventions may enhance the treatment and may even be crucial at times, only a consistent one-on-one relationship provides the nurturance and stability that the patient is likely to need. Individualized ongoing therapy with a single clinician gives the patient the undivided attention that he or she requires and is the core of treatment.

The ego of a person susceptible to psychosis is too easily fragmented to tolerate large, uninterrupted doses of family treatment—with its potential for conflict and ambiguity. The patient needs the steadying predictability of individual psychotherapy. In the following case, the therapist underestimated the importance of a one-on-one relationship.

> For several months, a mental health trainee had been providing weekly therapy to a thirty-two-year-old seamstress who worked at home. The patient lived with her parents and a younger brother. In her only hospitalization several years before, she had been diagnosed as chronically schizophrenic. Although rarely leaving home, the patient came regularly and punctually to her clinic appointments.

The trainee arranged for occasional family meetings that included the patient's parents and younger brother. The trainee discussed the case with his supervisor. In analyzing the case, they agreed that the parents appeared emotionally overinvolved with their daughter and that the patient's illness deflected attention from the parents' marital problems.

The supervisor persuaded the trainee to present the case to a nationally known family therapist at a clinical conference in a nearby city. The family agreed to participate. After the demonstration interview, the visiting expert elucidated the dynamics of the family system and recommended continuing family treatment.

Persuaded by the logic of this assessment, the trainee reconceptualized his patient's problems. He now understood them as embedded within the family and therefore no longer amenable to individual treatment. He scheduled the family for weekly therapy. They showed up a few times, but then the patient refused to attend. Finally, only the parents showed up. Shortly afterward, the patient decompensated and was admitted to the state hospital.

Unlike the therapist in the case just cited, who virtually—albeit unintentionally—abandoned his patient, the therapist in the next case sustained her one-on-one relationship with the patient while also establishing ongoing contact with the family. The following case illustrates how the course of individual and family treatment fluctuates, depending on where the patient is in the clinical continuum from acute illness to relative health. At times, psychosis may preclude family therapy, whereas at other times, when the patient is not psychotic and functioning, family or couples therapy is a valuable component of treatment.

A married twenty-eight-year-old woman was brought by her husband to a walk-in clinic because of emerging psychosis. She had a severe postpartum depression after the birth of her first child and had recovered, but she was now withdrawing and avoiding contact with her second, eight-month-old child. The clinician who interviewed the patient identified the symptoms as similar to those that occurred during the first depression. She provided crisis intervention, arranged for appropriate medication, and provided support for the husband in his role as caregiver for the children. Subsequently, the clinician established a therapeutic relationship with the woman that deepened over the several months that the patient attended the clinic.

The patient's psychosis cleared, and she resumed her normal, highly conscientious pattern of attentive mothering. During therapy following the psychosis, she shamefully confessed that when sick, she had beaten her first child so hard that the baby's skin had broken and bled: "I thought the Devil was in her. I had to beat the Devil out of her." As the patient's recovery continued, she felt herself ready to resume a teaching career and went on to manage a full-time job, as well as handling the responsibilities of motherhood and leading a church choir. Her medication was gradually discontinued and she terminated therapy, but she was encouraged to remain in touch.

After several months, she recontacted the therapist to ask for marital therapy. The therapist met with her and her husband twice. Every issue they raised involved their children and appeared to be appropriate for couples counseling. However, recalling the patient's earlier discussion about her fear of an "evil spirit" affecting the children, the therapist suggested putting the marital therapy "on hold" in order to have several individual meetings with the mother. In those individual meetings, the patient acknowledged racing thoughts of her family's impending destruction. As a result, couples treatment was postponed and the patient resumed individual treatment and medication.

After several weeks, she recompensated. She was sustained for several years with individual treatment interspersed with couples counseling. The marital therapy helped the patient see that she could relinquish some responsibility for the children to her husband and still be a good mother.

6. *In general, encourage relatives to communicate with you in the presence of the patient. Avoid communicating with family members without the patient's knowledge unless absolutely necessary.* One of the trickiest aspects of working with potentially paranoid, psychosis-prone patients is handling unsolicited communications from relatives about problems at home. Generally, the therapist is reluctant to communicate with the family behind the patient's back because that smacks of conspiracy. The solution to this problem is to insist on communicating with family members in front of the patient as much as possible. As long as the patient is not dangerously psychotic, most topics that relatives raise are ones that lend themselves to discussion in family meetings. Encouraging relatives to air complaints in front of the patient in the therapist's office encourages families to solve problems together. It also exposes them to the therapist's example of how to communicate constructively in times of conflict. When family meetings occur regularly (monthly, for example), patients view them as part of the treatment routine, rather than as suspicion-arousing evidence of trouble at home. Family members, in turn, count on the meetings to serve as a forum in which to express their concerns.

The next case is an example of combining individual and family treatment in such a way that troubleshooting occurs within the framework of ongoing therapy.

A twenty-seven-year-old male warehouse worker who lived with his parents had begun weekly individual therapy while still attending a day hospital. His parents had described his behavior at home before his inpatient hospitalization as belligerent and disruptive. Diagnosed as schizophrenic, he had been taking medication reluctantly but regularly for several months, and his behavior had changed. At outpatient family meetings with his therapist, he related to his parents in a compliant manner.

Privately, though, he told his therapist that he objected to his father's telling him what to do, insisting that "he treats me like a dog in training." He complained about his father's putting pressure on him to get to work in the morning, and in fact the patient's attendance at the warehouse had begun to decline. When his therapist asked him about this, basing his comments on a report from a vocational counselor, the patient angrily snapped, "My father's been telling you that! That's how you know!" The therapist explained that he had had no contact with his parents outside of the family meetings that the patient himself attended.

Soon afterward, the patient's mother called to say that her son was sleeping poorly and had been wandering the streets late at night. The therapist invited the parents to join with the patient at a meeting the next day. At that meeting, the patient admitted that he had stopped taking his medication. He agreed to start again, and in time his mental status improved. Subsequently, the patient and his parents continued to meet with the therapist. The clinician worked with them on family interactions, particularly on how to handle the early morning hours before the patient had to go to work.

In contrast to the preceding case, the one that follows is an example of botched communication. Here a therapist found herself in an extremely awkward position vis-à-vis her patient and the patient's family.

A twenty-seven-year-old woman who worked as a part-time librarian was in individual treatment for over a year. The patient also attended weekly group therapy. Although only transiently psychotic in the past, she had three long hospitalizations and had been involved with the mental health system for several years. Her parents were active in the local chapter of a family-based national advocacy organization for the mentally ill. When the therapist requested an opportunity to meet with her mother and father, the patient adamantly refused and spent many sessions venting anger at her parents.

After eventually leaving home to live by herself, the patient described fights at home when she returned to visit, mainly about money and the small amount of support her family was providing. Around this time, the therapist began to receive telephone messages from the mother but did not return the calls. One day, the therapist received a letter from the mother saying that she had been trying to reach her. The mother expressed concern about conflict with her daughter and requested a family meeting. The therapist called the mother and said that she would talk with her daughter about the possibility of a four-way meeting that would include the patient and her parents.

At the next session of individual therapy, the patient entered angrily and confronted the therapist about talking to her mother without her permission. Soon afterward, she "fired" the therapist and vehemently complained about her in group therapy.

In this example, the patient refused to let her therapist contact her parents. Given that the situation was not an emergency, the therapist made a mistake in initiating a call to the mother without first discussing it with her patient. However, in examining this case over its entire course, an alternative strategy becomes apparent. When the therapy first started, the therapist could have made it clear that helping her patient involved getting to know what her parents were like and how they interacted with their daughter. The therapist might have spoken of her patient's need for financial support from her parents and suggested negotiating for that during a family meeting at which the therapist would act as her patient's advocate.

In summary, the therapist could probably have identified reasons for involving the family that the patient would have experienced as ego syntonic. Generally, such persuasion is effective if the therapist has formed a relationship with the patient and if the patient anticipates that in any encounter with the family, the therapist will be an ally.

7. *Obtain prior permission from the patient to communicate directly with the family in emergency situations.* If a currently nonpsychotic patient has a history of psychotic episodes, the therapist and the patient need to discuss the possibility of relapse. The talk should not only focus on how to prevent another relapse but also on how to intervene at early stages and what to do if it cannot be stopped. These discussions should include any close family members who have helped in the past to deal with the patient's psychotic episodes. The therapist should ask the patient for permission to communicate with them directly in the event of a future recurrence of psychosis (Atwood, Mushrush, and Gutheil, 1987).

In the following case, a clinician worked with her patient and his wife to develop a contract that set the ground rules for dealing with incipient psychosis.

> A psychiatrist had been treating a thirty-two-year-old married sales manager for manic episodes. After a third hospitalization, the patient was stabilized on lithium, returned to work, and was asymptomatic. His therapist met with him individually on a regular basis and also held monthly meetings with him and his wife.
>
> The therapist suggested to the couple that they plan together for early intervention in case he became symptomatic again. The doctor asked them to identify early warning signs of relapse based on their previous experience during his breakdowns. They made up a list of behaviors that mainly occurred at home and therefore could not be observed by the therapist. Next, the three of them wrote a contract that said that if any of these behaviors were to happen, the wife was to ask her husband to tell the therapist. If he balked, she was to telephone the doctor or come to a therapy session to tell the therapist herself.
>
> Conversely, if the therapist suspected an impending relapse, she was to call the wife to see if she had corroborative data. If a relapse seemed likely and the husband was uncooperative, then the wife and the therapist were to work together to get him evaluated and appropriately treated, including confining him in a hospital if necessary.

Patient, wife, and therapist signed this contract, and for several months he remained asymptomatic. Gradually, however, his mood changed, and his therapist noticed that he was unusually tense at his biweekly appointment. Shortly afterward, the clinician received an urgent request from his wife for a three-way meeting.

When they met, the wife told the therapist that her husband had cleaned the bathroom several times and was reading the Bible aloud. Both behaviors appeared on their list of warning signals. The psychiatrist adjusted the medication and set up call-in hours and extra appointments for the week ahead. During that week, the doctor called the patient's wife at work to find out how her husband was doing at home. In time he recompensated, and both husband and wife expressed satisfaction about having avoided hospitalization.

8. *Do not secretly or suddenly conspire with the family to exercise control over the patient.* Psychiatric hospitalizations are among the most stressful experiences that clinicians who work with patients vulnerable to psychosis face. Many a treatment relationship falters or falls apart completely because the therapist inadvertently alienates a potentially out-of-control patient or has trouble dealing with distraught family members. The following case illustrates the kind of dilemmas that such a situation presents.

A forty-one-year-old female high school teacher was being treated in individual therapy. She lived in a small apartment in the home of her brother and sister-in-law. Several years earlier, she had been hospitalized for a single depressive psychotic episode. During her three months of therapy, the patient had become increasingly agitated about her relationship with a fellow teacher she had dated for several years. To her despair, he precipitously broke off the relationship to marry another woman. Although frequently tearful, sleeping poorly, and losing weight, the patient managed to continue teaching, appeared to improve on medication, and did not become psychotic. She spent time on weekends with her brother's eight-year-old daughter and expressed much affection for the little girl.

However, the patient later began to miss days at work and told her therapist about wanting to end the pain. Hearing this, the therapist suggested hospitalization. The patient vigorously refused, saying that she had hated being hospitalized and was determined to finish the semester that was about to end. As the patient had no plan to hurt herself and appeared able to work, the therapist decided not to force hospitalization. She told the patient that she would support her efforts to stay out of the hospital as long as her condition did not get worse.

That evening, the patient's brother placed an urgent call to the therapist to express his and his wife's serious concern about his sister's behavior. It was similar to what it had been before the overdose that led to her previous hospitalization. Feeling alarmed, the therapist invited the brother and his wife to the clinic the next day and scheduled them for the same time as the patient's appointment.

When the four of them met, the patient was startled by the unexpected visitors. She became taut with anger but remained silent. The therapist permitted the couple to express their opinions and feelings about the patient's behavior and why hospitalization was necessary. The therapist said that she too had come to realize that hospitalization was needed. The patient listened but continued to say nothing, breaking down only when her sister-in-law said that her niece no longer wanted to spend time with her. At that point the patient, in tears, agreed to hospitalization and arrangements were made. On her way to the waiting ambulance, she said, "This is so humiliating."

Weeks later, after hearing nothing from the patient or the hospital, the therapist made inquiries. She was told that her former patient had been discharged following a brief hospitalization and had requested another outpatient therapist.

The management of this case called for exercising judgment in the face of a fluctuating clinical picture. Whether or not the patient required hospitalization is less an issue here than the fact that the therapist lost control of the case and turned the decision making over to the family. Involving the family occurred too late, after the situation at home had already gotten out of hand. The family had been left unsupported to deal with the patient's serious depression. Their anxiety was allowed to mount until it reached an intolerable level, at which point they contacted the therapist. Their anxiety resonated with the therapist's, leading to the confrontation at the family meeting that left the patient feeling isolated and betrayed.

There is no easy way to handle a hospitalization. However, the process is more likely to go smoothly if the patient and the family are helped to experience hospitalization as the end point of an evolving, monitored process. Under this circumstance, the necessity for hospitalization gradually becomes clear to everybody, rather than being seen as an abrupt expunging of the patient after a period of miscommunication and confusion.

9. *Work with the family, as well as with the patient, to plan for and carry out any major changes that take place in the patient's life. Do not unilaterally make arrangements with the patient to change his or her life without including the family in the planning and decision making.* When patients live with their families, any major change that happens in the life of the patient will affect the family. Similarly, how the family responds to the patient as change occurs will have an impact on the patient. The patient will cope with change more easily if the family supports it. The ego of a person vulnerable to psychosis is likely to be too weak to survive a change that the family opposes, no matter how supportive the therapist may be.

In the following case, a therapist encouraged his patient to take a seemingly appropriate step toward rehabilitation. However, the therapist failed initially to bring the parents along in this process. Once he did this and the parents themselves became supportive of change, the patient's progress proceeded on firmer ground.

A twenty-five-year-old man had remained unemployed following his discharge from an institution for the criminally insane, to which he had been committed at age eighteen after stabbing a neighbor. The only child of retired parents with whom he lived, he spent his days reading electronics manuals, helping his father tend the yard, and accompanying his mother to the supermarket. He took antipsychotic medicine—his diagnosis was chronic paranoid schizophrenia—and had begun individual therapy.

Soon after treatment began, his therapist encouraged him to enter vocational training, and he began a full-time program at a sheltered workshop. Although able to handle tasks competently, the patient became convinced that fellow workers and neighbors were watching him constantly. One night during a week when his therapist was on vacation, he cut his wrist in the bathroom at home, almost severing a tendon.

In the aftermath of this serious suicide attempt, he told his therapist why he had cut himself. He described being filled with unbearable shame about being observed through his bedroom window masturbating, although in actuality his room was on the third floor and not visible to neighbors. He was so ashamed, he said, that he could not face waking up his parents to tell them that he was suicidal.

The therapist, realizing his omission in not involving the patient's parents, invited them to the clinic for the first of several family meetings that occurred intermittently with individual therapy. The parents said that they had disapproved of their son's starting at the workshop and had tried to discourage him from attending. They said that they thought that a five-day work-week was much too taxing for their son.

From then on, the therapist used family meetings as a place where changes—big and small—were discussed. Eventually, the parents supported their son's attending a day treatment program after visiting it themselves. He finally returned to the workshop on a three-day-a-week basis.

As this case suggests, the therapist needs to devote time and effort to seeing that the family understands the reason for change, what it implies for the patient and for them, and what role they can play in helping the patient adjust. As in everything else that the therapist does with the family, the goal is to engage the family as collaborators in the treatment of the patient.

Summary

Successfully combining individual and family treatment for psychosis-prone outpatients who live with their families is a process of keeping the needs of the patient and the family in balance. The therapist has to respond to each in an evenhanded way that preserves an alliance with both. Through guidelines and case reports, this chapter describes how to maintain that balance.

The therapist-patient relationship is the core of treatment and keeps the clinician's focus squarely on the individual needs of the patient. In keeping with that focus, the therapist encourages self-determination on the patient's part and sets up opportunities for the family to communicate directly with the therapist in front of the patient, rather than surreptitiously behind the patient's back. In keeping with a collateral emphasis on the family, the therapist involves the family regularly and early in the course of treatment, respects the family's knowledge of the patient, puts that knowledge to use, and works with the family to deal promptly and effectively with incipient emergencies.

The therapist knows that it is not only the therapist but also the family who stimulate a patient to change. The therapist, building on whatever strengths the patient and family possess, enlists the family as an ally in promoting and bringing about therapeutic progress.

References

Anderson, C. M., Reiss, D. J., and Hogarty, G. E. *Schizophrenia and the Family.* New York: Guilford Press, 1986.

Atwood, N. "Integrating Individual and Family Treatment for Outpatients Vulnerable to Psychosis." *American Journal of Psychotherapy,* 1990, *44,* 247–254.

Atwood, N., Mushrush, G., and Gutheil, T. G. "Forum." *Newsletter of the Massachusetts Psychiatric Society,* 1987, *23*(5), 7–8.

Bernheim, K. F., and Lehman, A. F. *Working with Families of the Mentally Ill.* New York: Norton, 1985.

Davenport, Y. B., and Adland, M. L. "Issues in the Treatment of the Married Bipolar Patient: Denial and Dependency." In M. R. Lansky (ed.), *Family Approaches to Major Psychiatric Disorders.* Washington, D.C.: American Psychiatric Association Press, 1985.

Dearth, N., Labenski, B. J., Mott, M. E., and Pellegrini, L. M. *Families Helping Families.* New York: Norton, 1986.

De Nour, A. K. "Psychosocial Aspects of the Management of Mania." In R. H. Belmaker and H. M. Van Praag (eds.), *Mania: An Evolving Concept.* Jamaica, N.Y.: SP Medical and Scientific Books, 1980.

Group for the Advancement of Psychiatry. *A Family Affair: Helping Families Cope with Mental Illness.* Report no. 119. New York: Brunner/Mazel, 1986.

Intagliata, J., Wilner, B., and Egri, G. "Role of the Family in Case Management of the Mentally Ill." *Schizophrenia Bulletin,* 1986, *12,* 699–708.

Jamison, K. R. "Psychotherapeutic Issues and Suicide Prevention in the Treatment of Bipolar Disorders." In R. E. Hales and A. J. Frances (eds.), *Psychiatric Update: The American Psychiatric Association Annual Review.* Vol. 6. Washington, D.C.: American Psychiatric Association Press,1987.

Johnson, D. L. "The Family's Experience of Living with Mental Illness." In H. P. Lefley and D. L. Johnson (eds.), *Families as Allies in the Treatment of the Mentally Ill: New Directions for Mental Health Professionals.* Washington, D.C.: American Psychiatric Press, 1990.

Roberts, R. "The Outpatient Treatment of Schizophrenia: An Integrated and Comprehensive Management-Oriented Approach." *Psychiatric Quarterly,* 1984, *56,* 91–112.

NANCY C. ATWOOD, a clinical social worker, has worked as a psychotherapist, emergency room clinician, and supervisor in outpatient mental health settings in Massachusetts. She is on the adjunct faculty at Smith College School for Social Work and has a private practice in Boston and Wellesley, Massachusetts.

4

Belief in the biological roots of mental illness will govern some of what we do in a psychiatric rehabilitation program.

The Biological Basis of Mental Illness

Jerry Dincin

No tenet of psychiatric rehabilitation holds more importance than the centrality of the biological basis of mental illness. From this basic understanding stems the focus on preventing hospitalization via medication compliance. The understanding of the role of biology in mental illness is important not only in and of itself but also in combating the stigma attached to mental illness and the resulting frequent denial of mental illness by rehabilitative agency members. At Thresholds, the response to the centrality of biological causes is three-pronged: medication education, medication prescription, and medication compliance.

Biological Illness Requires Biological Treatment

The definition of mental illness that I gave in a 1989 speech in Miami and later adapted for a *Psychosocial Rehabilitation Journal* article still holds validity for me, "Most mental illness starts with a genetic defect, accidental or inherited, which predisposes a person to a significant bio-chemical disturbance in brain neurotransmitter functioning. An extremely low tolerance for stress, either of biological or psychological origin, can trigger the exacerbation of symptoms, but is not itself causal. This altered biochemistry leads to distortions in 'normal' perceptions, emotions, behavior, intellect, and other brain functions that collectively we term 'mental illness.'"

Without this change in brain biochemistry, we would not see the symptoms we call mental illness. It is therefore absolutely basic that we try to restore a more "correct" brain chemistry so that symptoms will be reduced and members' behavior will return to what our Western culture has decided is "normal." This restoration is accomplished through the intelligent, sensitive, knowledgeable administration of medications that help correct brain chemistry gone awry.

Occasionally, perhaps too frequently, medications are prescribed by people without sensitivity to the member or to the side effects the medications cause. Sometimes they are administered by mean-spirited and punitive personnel. Sometimes they are administered by people without intelligence or caring. I make no defense of these people except to say that sometimes symptoms are so disruptive and outrageous (which of course is not the "fault" of the patient) that heavy medication or restraints seem the only course possible. Poor administration is never excusable and must be corrected by careful monitoring of personnel and their attitudes, habits, and behavior. However, even the overuse or misuse of medications does not change the basic truth as I see it: mental illness is essentially biological and almost always needs to be corrected by biological means (in other words, medications).

At this point, the best thinking of scientists I respect indicates that mental illness lies in some defect in the dopamine or serotonin (or both) systems. And it appears dopamine receptors are the key to understanding these defects. Although there are five receptors, the two most important are D-2 and D-4 and their interactions with the serotonin systems. Although all this is subject to change as science brings us more insight, what we do know now is that medication works: it affects those dysfunctional sites in the brain. What we do not know for sure and what we need to keep an open mind on is this: Is there a developmental error or a gap in early neurological development, and if so, is the cause a genetic malfunction, as suggested in my definition, or a virus or something else?

What is also not yet well understood is the interaction between biology and psychology—that is, what is the effect of psychological trauma on brain biology? Perhaps for some people, the psychological trauma inherent in sexual or physical abuse or other environmental harm is so severe that it actually changes neurotransmitter chemistry in the brain. Although the jury is still out on that issue, we need to take this possibility seriously and be willing to alter our treatment protocol accordingly. Perhaps a lesser reliance on medication (although I expect that some would be beneficial) and a greater reliance on psychotherapy, hypnosis, Holotropic Breathwork, and psychosynthesis is in order for persons whose symptoms emanate from sexual abuse or other psychological trauma. Another question is whether street drugs like PCP and LSD can cause mental illness. I believe that although they can mimic schizophrenia, the effects of these drugs are transient unless the drug user is biologically prone to schizophrenia.

Of course, a person can have genetic defects and therefore mental illness to a slight, moderate, or severe degree, just as is the case with other illnesses. But at psychiatric rehabilitation centers, staff rarely see people with mild cases of schizophrenia. They see people who are at least moderately and usually severely and persistently affected.

Why is it so important that we have a causation hypothesis of mental illness? It is our understanding of the cause of mental illness that tells us what to do about that illness. Our rehabilitation program flows out of our hypothesis. If we believe schizophrenia is totally psychological in origin, caused by familial interactions in childhood, then the remedial course of action will be some form of psychotherapy. However, mental illness has been with humanity for a very long time. And from earliest recorded Western history, people with mental illness have suffered for their bizarre behavior. They have been excluded from towns, depicted as passengers on a "ship of fools," whirled in revolving chairs, chained, bound in wet sheets, and burned as witches. In more modern times, insulin shock, psychoanalysis, Laingian therapy, vitamin therapy, and lobotomy have all been tried, with modest or no effects. Electroconvulsive therapy (ECT) definitely does help some people but can have devastating side effects and is now used less frequently. The only treatment in the history of mankind that has shown consistent scientifically verifiable improvement over placebo is the use of the medications currently available. Nothing even approaches the consistent usefulness of medication in reducing the symptoms of this devastating illness. We do not know how to cure it, but we do know how to make the symptoms tolerable for most people.

Medication has been the single most potent force in emptying the hospitals from their highest use in the 1950s to the present. If not for the discovery of antipsychotic medications, is there any serious doubt that these hospitals would still be crammed with patients? Nothing else made a significant difference. Civil rights cases and exposés of inhumane hospital treatment, the family movement, and mental health legislation would have had little if any effect on the mental hospital population if medication had not made it possible for the heretofore intractable mentally ill to leave these institutions successfully.

I believe, therefore, that mental illness exists and has existed for all of recorded time. I reject the views of Thomas Szasz and his supporters, who deny the existence of mental illness. Nor do I believe that psychiatrists and the medical profession invented mental illness. History tells us that it has always been with us in both mild and severe forms. Although it is true that some cultures revere those whom we would call mentally ill, in Western culture the symptoms of mental illness are regarded as aberrant and undesirable.

The acceptance of the biological understanding of mental illness leads us directly to the first goal of psychiatric rehabilitation: keeping people out of the hospital. For psychiatric rehabilitation practitioners, acting on this goal boils down to helping members understand the need to take medication and then actually taking it. No amount of talk therapy, group therapy, or visits with a psychiatrist will repair a biological problem in the brain. The biological side *must* be attended to as the first step in rehabilitation. Everything in a comprehensive psychiatric rehabilitation program like that at Thresholds flows from that premise. My experience has taught me again and again that many, if not most, hospitalizations are preventable. Yearly studies at Thresholds verify this observation. Forty to 60 percent of all rehospitalizations of Thresholds members are in some way related to a failure in medication compliance. Reduction of the compliance problem will dramatically reduce hospitalizations.

Issues in Medication Compliance

Members have many reasons for not taking prescribed medication: denial of illness, medication side effects, poor self-image, medication ineffectiveness, a feeling of "I'm well now," and particularly among members in a manic phase, enjoyment of the symptoms of the illness.

Each of these reasons (and the others listed later in this chapter) needs to be addressed with members. Most important, staff must assist members to understand that medication compliance is central to their rehabilitation and to building a new life outside the hospital. For us to ignore medication compliance or to let others take care of medication issues is to abrogate our responsibilities as caring professionals. Sometimes I think agencies that do not pay close attention to medication issues, either for philosophical or practical reasons, believe there is no such thing as mental illness.

By the time the members at Thresholds begin psychiatric rehabilitation, they are no longer in the early stage of mental illness but usually have had many episodes and frequent hospitalizations. Staff owe it to these long-time sufferers to help them adhere to their prescribed medication. Obviously, the majority of members have the final say in whether they take medication. But staff need to be persuasive in teaching members about medication, and to be persuasive, staff must know what they are talking about from a moral and a scientific perspective.

Although it is not impossible to work with people who are not taking medication, if they are very symptomatic they tend to gain little from the program. In a very few situations, Thresholds will terminate a member if his or her symptoms are so severe that it is obvious staff are wasting their time and the member's time—for example, a member whose full-blown paranoid or manic symptoms are intolerable or whose behavior is so destructive that he or she cannot function in the Thresholds community. At such times, staff may initiate or encourage hospitalization, change to another type of programming, or tell the member he or she cannot stay in the program as it is structured. But these situations are the exceptions to the rule. Exclusion from Thresholds for medication noncompliance happens rarely.

There are at least three major problems with psychotropic medications that are not yet resolved.

First, any medication that affects brain chemistry to control the symptoms of mental illness will also have secondary effects. Even mild secondary effects are uncomfortable, and the more severe ones can be unbearable. Part of psychiatric rehabilitation is to help the member decide whether the basic effect of the medication on the symptoms is worth the discomfort of the secondary effects. Most of the time, it makes sense to lean toward supporting the basic effect of the medication, because too often the alternative is hospitalization. However, this basic decision is not ours, but the members'.

Because side, or secondary, effects are a plague for members and are the single most important reason for members' discontinuing their medication,

they need to be taken seriously by mental health professionals who are knowledgeable, alert to their occurrence, and able to act as advocates with the pre-
scribing psychiatrist in those cases where members cannot express themselves
adequately or are unaware of the side effect. A regular screening for the side
effect of tardive dyskinesia (TD) should be performed by psychiatric rehabilitation line staff, who should then report any slight TD symptom to the psychiatrist for further evaluation. Side effects are *the* major problem in
medication compliance.

Also, pharmaceutical companies need to continue their efforts to invent
medications that will target the precise symptoms of mental illness with
fewer secondary effects. Indeed, this has happened over the years: clozap-
ine, Risperidone, valproic acid, and Prozac are all significant improvements
over prior medications. Personally, I am continually grateful that pharmaceutical companies have come up with all these improvements since 1954,
and I hope they continue to do so.

Second, every person's reaction to medication is idiosyncratic as to the
most effective medication or combination of medications and the correct
dosage. And every person's reaction to secondary effects is different. This
makes the administration of medication subject to trial and error, a kind of
scientific art form. Medication should be administered by experts who keep
up with the scientific literature and yet are willing to make intelligent,
humane "guesses" at what is best. Amateur practitioners (family doctors)
are usually not well suited for this task, but psychologists could and should
be trained for this important responsibility. Finding the right combination
of medications to control symptoms and control side effects over an
extended period is a difficult job.

Third, known medications unfortunately do not work for some people,
or they work only modestly or engender an allergic response, leaving people with too many symptoms to operate effectively. This is as sad as the situation of people with severe infections who cannot tolerate any antibiotics.
Just as frustrating is the situation of the people for whom medications work
well initially but then lose effectiveness over time (in the film *Awakenings,*
Robert De Niro touchingly portrayed the tragedy of temporarily effective
medication). Again, we must turn to the pharmaceutical firms to keep working on this.

Program for Medication Compliance

A psychiatric rehabilitation program should include a program for medication compliance. The components of the Thresholds medication compliance
program illustrate the many elements that go into such an effort:

Teach the biological basis of mental illness. Members can and should come
to understand the biological basis of mental illness. Group and individual
education sessions geared to a simple explanation of the biological basis of
mental illness help relieve members' sense of guilt at being ill. Issues of grief

and loss of potential may then arise, but they are easier to deal with than denial of mental illness, which creates a plethora of problems.

Develop a medication education class. Members should understand precisely what medications they are taking, why they are taking them, and how the medications work. They should also understand why the medications have side effects, and staff can help members process their tolerance of those side effects. The Thresholds medication group, for example, is an eight-week, one-hour-per-week class led by a social worker. Thresholds does not have a psychiatrist running this group primarily because of the expense, but a psychiatrist usually leads one class. Each session is run as a class: notes are taken and tests are given at the end of the session. All members participate in this group.

Develop an individualized prodromal pattern for every member. Staff need information on each member's unique collection of prodromes, warning signs that are yet not full-blown symptoms. Prodromes might include increased irritability, sleeplessness, or changes in appetite or personal cleanliness. Sometimes prodromes are more spectacular, such as sudden moves to other states, but usually staff need to be alert to slight precursors to an increasingly symptomatic picture. Once a person is paranoid or manic, we are no longer talking about prodromal patterns. At Thresholds, staff try to get an initial prodromal pattern during the intake process. This information is asked first of the members themselves when they are in a stable state, but by far the best source of prodromal information is parents. Other tips on prodromes can be gathered from staff, friends, and hospital records.

Work on improving the relationship between the member and the doctor, as necessary. Occasionally, members do not like their psychiatrist or do not know how to talk to him or her. These members can be taught how to communicate more effectively with their doctor. This process sometimes requires staff participation in the doctor-member interview to make sure the doctor really hears the member's report, and in turn, the member hears and understands the doctor's report.

Use testimonials and other peer supports from medication compliant members and former members. Despite caseworkers' best attempts, members may not believe what they say about medication. However, these members may more readily listen to and respond to other members. Peer support should therefore be used as much as possible.

Use community meetings to support medication compliance. At Thresholds, community meetings of members support medication compliance, as do occasional focus groups on medication.

Analyze precisely any resistance to medication, especially denial of mental illness. In both individual and group encounters, staff need to work with members to reduce medication resistance. Essentially, nobody likes to take medication for any reason. For people with a history of mental illness, the resistance is even more pointed, and staff need to help patients see the analogies to purely physical illness. Denial of mental illness is the most difficult issue psychiatric rehabilitation staff will face. Although I do not have a lot of advice on this, I can suggest that one technique that sometimes leads to a breakthrough is to ask members themselves to explain the origin of their symptoms and of their multiple hospitalizations and unusual behavior; ask them to name a cause.

Offer parents of members medication education and solicit their support. Because family and friends can exert much influence on members, support groups for them should help them understand the centrality of medication compliance and the biological basis of mental illness. Parents' support can be crucial; their lack of support devastating.

Develop and use relationship. Relationship is *the* crucial factor in medication compliance. A trusting relationship between member and staff remains the best long-term method of maintaining medication compliance.

Deal seriously with side effects. Members have some important reasons for not maintaining medication compliance. In surveys of Thresholds members, as mentioned earlier, the single most important reason for noncompliance is side effects. They must be dealt with as they arise and should not be ignored under any circumstance. Members can understand taking special medication just for their side effects. In certain cases, staff will have to assist members in tolerating side effects. A useful analogy is that the treatment for certain cancers may feel awful, but it is worth it to maintain life. Thresholds staff are taught to do tardive dyskinesia screening (using the Dyskinesia Identification System: Condensed User Scale [DISCUS]), and prompt referrals to doctors are made if warranted. Staff must always be vigilant in watching for side effects.

Analyze history of noncompliance through hospital records. It is important for staff to discuss with members the prior noncompliant experiences that have led to rehospitalization. This examination may also show what could have been done differently to increase compliance.

Start a special group for all members hospitalized three or more times. This group will focus on attitudinal issues, which might include these frequently expressed member attitudes about medication:

"I feel better without meds."
"Its 'just' symptom control and doesn't effect a basic 'cure.'"
"I no longer need meds."
"Meds do not help."
"The voices said to stop meds."
"The symptoms are better so I stopped."
"I want to test myself to see if I really need the meds."
"I want to try and do it on my own."
"I am afraid of taking it for the rest of my life."
"I want to be natural."
"I can't think as clearly with meds."

In addition, patients may make statements that indicate

- Fears of dependency, addiction, or loss of control
- Fears of harm to body or offspring
- A sense of stigma or embarrassment at having to take meds
- A dislike of the idea of taking meds
- A lack of understanding of the medication's preventive function
- Experiences of loss of creativity
- Experiences of forgetting to take all the doses
- A desire to "get back" at the therapist by misusing medication
- Experiences of medication's interfering with sexual desire or potency

These and other statements and attitudes form the agenda for discussion in the medication attitude group.

Recognize members who stay out of the hospital for a specific length of time. Every year, Thresholds throws a party to celebrate members who remained out of the hospital for a year or more. On these Member Recognition Days, honorees receive certificates, are publicly praised, and receive the applause of their peers. Catered food is offered, and family members, friends, and doctors are invited.

Pay attention to any substance abuse that relates to medication compliance. If substance abuse is inhibiting a member from taking medication, seek a consultation with the member's psychiatrist. Sometimes, mixing street drugs and medication matters a great deal; at other times, it does not.

Make videos of members when they are well. These videos can then be shown to members when they get symptomatic, and vice versa.

Achieve a high level of staff training and commitment to the entire compliance program. As a part of this training, discuss problems with medication compliance and techniques for achieving it at regular staff meetings.

Accompany members to their appointments with the psychiatrist. Also, employ doctors who will make home visits when necessary.

Make a written agreement with each member, at intake or thereafter, that he or she will take prescribed medication.

Make sure there are funds for medication. Have staff get prescriptions filled if necessary.

Develop the best schedule of taking medication for each member. To help members maintain their schedules, use pill boxes or other reminder mechanisms, including prepackaged medications; use injectable medication as frequently as practical (if necessary, use a visiting nurse to give members injectable medication at home); use lab tests to analyze blood levels of medication.

Role of the Psychiatrist in Medication Compliance

When working with the chronically mentally ill, our senior psychiatrist considers it essential to be connected with an agency. The chronically mentally ill person has a complex package of problems, and the person working in a private practice will find it too difficult to take these problems on alone.

Thresholds uses members' psychiatrists in a targeted manner. None are on staff salary and none have any operational say in daily Thresholds activity; instead, they are treated as consultants. It is valuable to have as much of this consulting as possible done at the agency, otherwise communication suffers. It is much easier to speak with a psychiatrist about a member for a minute at Thresholds than to wend through a maze of answering services and beepers. Of course, many members maintain their own psychiatrists, as is their option, and Thresholds staff do not attempt to change these doctors.

In a psychiatric rehabilitation program with a mandate to avoid hospitalizations, psychiatrists need to be readily available to handle emergencies. If a staff person or a member realizes that the member is beginning to reach the point of hospitalization, our doctors are never far away. Psychiatrists are also valuable for the expert training they can be paid to provide to line staff. Such training sessions can cover general medication orientation, new medications, biological causes of mental illness, medications' side effects, and tardive dyskinesia screens.

And of course, psychiatrists are valuable in helping staff maintain medication compliance and for imparting specific professional knowledge to line and supervisory staff.

Absolutely nothing is more important in psychiatric rehabilitation than medication compliance. All our pearls of wisdom, caring, and love will not be useful unless supported by an intelligent, sophisticated, sensitive, and humane medication management and medication compliance program.

Renaming Mental Illness

Finally, once the basis of mental illness is understood to be biological, it becomes apparent that a new name for mental illness would be appropriate, one that reflects its cause. I suggest *neurotransmitter/stress syndrome*. That name would be particularly helpful as a substitute for *schizophrenia*, a term that has long outlived its usefulness. *Schizo* is now used as a derogatory term for almost any behavior we do not like or want to make fun of. Insensitive advertising, television show dialogue, and street jargon have stolen the true meaning of schizophrenic and made it into a curse word. The situation is reminiscent of the former use of *moron*, *imbecile*, and *idiot* to describe the three levels of mental retardation, terms that then came into daily conversation as pejorative descriptions of almost anyone. Isn't *Down's syndrome* much better as a name than any of its predecessors?

The name *neurotransmitter/stress syndrome* puts the emphasis on brain chemistry and also acknowledges that stress may precipitate the effect of defective chemistry.

JERRY DINCIN is executive director of Thresholds Psychiatric Rehabilitation Centers in Chicago.

5

*With sweeping changes in health care delivery shrinking
an already competitive therapist market, mental health
professionals are increasing their participation in the
forensic arena. The thread common to civil and criminal
psycholegal work is the challenge of testifying as an
expert witness.*

From Mental Health Professional to Expert Witness: Testifying in Court

Steven C. Bank

The recent explosive growth in the fields of forensic psychology and psychiatry attests to mental health professionals' changing role in response to an increasingly litigious society. Clinicians may participate in up to one million legal cases annually (Faust and Ziskin, 1988). Working on psycholegal issues such as child custody, insanity, and personal injury can be both challenging and frightening—particularly when you are subpoenaed to testify in court. Mental health professionals will find it easier to cope with the demands of providing expert testimony if they understand the spirit and development of our legal system.

What follows is an introduction to the adversarial process and a primer for navigating through both direct examination and cross-examination. The historical evolution of our legal system, the role of expert witnesses, and the basic elements of persuasive and ethical testimony are reviewed.

Introduction to the Adversary Process

People create laws to provide formal procedures for settling disputes so that societies are able to maintain order. By definition, any dispute is going to have opposing or what are called adversary positions. Hence the spirit and rules for U.S. courtrooms are collectively known as the *adversary process* (Kempin, 1973).

Within this confrontational setting, the judge or jury is asked to decide which lawyer's arguments sound more convincing or legally correct. When a mental health professional assumes the role of an expert witness, he or she becomes part of this adversarial process.

NEW DIRECTIONS FOR MENTAL HEALTH SERVICES, no. 91, Fall 2001   © John Wiley & Sons, Inc.

Trial by Ordeal. Historically, trial by battle and trial by ordeal predated civilized legal proceedings. In the twelfth century, the local laws of England allowed wealthy landowners to substitute champions to do judicial combat for them in settling disputes. Today attorneys champion the cause of their clients.

Before trial by jury, trial by ordeal was popular, although less so with defendants undergoing such litigation. The ordeals—an appeal to the supernatural to determine guilt or innocence—were frequently held during Church rituals at the high moment of the Mass. The ordeal of the hot iron involved having the accused carry a red-hot iron in his hand for a certain distance. If, after a set period of days, he had no marks on his hands, the accused was considered to be innocent. The ordeal of the cursed morsel entailed having the accused swallow a piece of dry bread with a feather in it. If the accused did not choke, he was considered to be innocent. Trial by ordeal could be easily manipulated (for example, by varying the heat of the iron or choosing the size of the feather) and was, therefore, ripe for corruption. In 1215, the Church of England forbade priests to participate in trials by ordeal. Consequently, the chief procedure for resolving criminal cases in England, that is, appeal to the supernatural, was eliminated.

Jurors as Witnesses. The option of allowing the judge to decide cases was rejected because he would be replacing the voice of God. It was agreed that villagers who had some acquaintance with the offense, or the offender, would help the court—and God—resolve the dispute.

The problem with this arrangement was that jurors served both as witnesses to the offense and as the body determining guilt or innocence. In addition, even those who accused the defendant of a crime could sit on the jury. It is understandable why most defendants were not eager to undergo trial by jury.

Approximately three hundred years later, the Elizabethan Act of 1562 created the statutory offense of perjury and also formalized our modern distinction between jurors and witnesses. The wheels of justice had spun full circle: whereas jurors were originally required to know all they could about a case, now they were to know nothing—until they listened to witnesses.

Competency of Witnesses to Testify. A basic concern under a system of trial by jury pertains to the competence of witnesses. The law recognizes that for a variety of reasons, not all witnesses may be either truthful or accurate. If the law is to discover the truth of a dispute, there must be some means to test or gauge the character and veracity of those who testify.

The grounds for finding a witness incompetent to testify have been developed over centuries. They were originally categorized under the now obsolete five I's of Interest, Insanity, Infancy, Infidelity, and Infamy. Holdsworth (1956, p. 98) states, "The canon law rejected the testimony of all males under fourteen and females under twelve, of the blind and the deaf and the dumb, of slaves, of infamous persons, and those convicted of crime, of excommunicated persons, of poor persons, and of women in criminal cases, of persons connected with either party by consanguinity and affinity, or belonging to the households of either party, of the enemies of either party, and of Jews, heretics, and pagans." Essentially, the only people remaining who qualified to testify as witnesses were wealthy male landowners.

Current practice dictates that—barring certain exceptions—virtually any individual with probative information can testify as a witness. Once the judge allows a witness to testify, his or her accuracy and truthfulness continues to be challenged through cross-examination, the essence of the adversary process.

The law can usually force a witness to answer almost any relevant question. The only constitutional exception is the Fifth Amendment right against self-incrimination. Certain witnesses can, however, withhold information acquired during confidential or privileged relationships.

Witnesses with Special Knowledge. Because of their special expertise and knowledge, mental health professionals establish confidential relationships. The same expertise that allows clinicians to form confidential relationships also permits them to testify in court as witnesses who are expert.

Written documentation of medical testimony in continental jurisprudence dates back to 1311 (Eigen and Andoll, 1986). Courts originally utilized expertise in two ways. First, jury members were selected *because* they had special knowledge or experience regarding the issue before the court. Second, skilled or knowledgeable people who were not jurors would assist the court by offering their opinion. The court would then decide what weight to give the opinion. It is this latter application of expert knowledge that is currently used because citizens can no longer serve in the dual role of juror and witness.

Today expert witnesses are either partisan or court appointed. A partisan expert who is retained by one litigant will likely undergo a more aggressive cross-examination than one who appears at the behest of the court.

Testimony: Fact Versus Opinion. There are two types of testimony that an expert witness can provide in court. He or she can testify either to questions of fact or to questions of opinion. Whereas the lay or nonexpert witness is restricted to testimony about facts (what he or she has directly experienced or observed), the expert witness (because of specialized knowledge and training) can offer the court opinions and conclusions.

When the expert testifies to opinions, he or she is only assisting the judge or jury, rather than establishing case facts. Whereas anyone can testify to observing a person clipping balloons to his head while screaming for the Mother Ship to pick him up, only an expert witness can offer opinions or conclusions as to whether the person was mentally ill at the time.

Witness Credibility. Whether the expert is testifying to facts or opinions, the adversary process presumes that the most effective way to determine the value of his or her testimony is by subjecting the expert to cross-examination. The outdated five I's of a witness's competence have been converted to contemporary issues of credibility.

In brief, the purpose of cross-examination is to bring forth any aspects of a witness's testimony that may be impeachable, that is, either inaccurate or biased. By testing the witness's credibility—whether the witness be lay or expert—jurors can most accurately appraise the value of his or her testimony. This, in turn, affords the court a greater opportunity to arrive at the truth.

Lawyers can attack an expert witness's credibility in at least five ways: by demonstrating that the witness made previous statements that are inconsistent with his or her current courtroom testimony, by arguing that the witness made errors in statement of fact, by convincing the court that the witness is biased and therefore not trustworthy, by showing that the expert does not possess the specific expertise needed for the case or that the methodology used to collect and analyze data is faulty, by attacking the general character of the witness. Common to all of the strategies for discrediting witnesses is the practice of stressing them. Taking the witness stand originally meant that the witness had to remain on his or her feet. There are still countries that force witnesses to stand while providing testimony in order to pressure them into revealing the truth.

Placing witnesses under emotional stress has traditionally been thought to facilitate unearthing the truth, and there is no doubt that cross-examination is designed to wear down those who take the stand. Unfamiliar courtroom rituals, procedures, and jargon are all stress factors embedded into the evolution of our legal system.

Dual Role of Expert Witnesses.   The term *expert witness* connotes two meanings and consequently two responsibilities for mental health professionals assuming that role. First, one must be expert, that is, authoritative or competent, in his or her chosen area of specialization. Second, the individual who participates as a witness needs to appreciate the huge difference between intellectual battle in the courtroom trenches versus the academic ivory tower. For an expert witness to be of value to the judge or jury, he or she must be an effective courtroom communicator (Bank and Poythress, 1982a).

There is no shortage of literature when it comes to advising experts on testifying (for example, Brodsky, 1977) and providing attorneys with strategies for cross-examination (for example, Ziskin and Faust, 1995). What remains under debate, however, concerns whether the proper role of the expert witness is that of educator, advocate, or adviser (Saks, 1990). Three arguments suggest that experts need to be persuasive advocates for their own opinions—which is fundamentally different from advocating for a litigant: you can be the foremost authority in the world in your chosen area of specialization, but if you cannot communicate your expertise in a clear and convincing fashion, then the value of your knowledge to a court will be severely limited. The lawyer performing cross-examination will attempt to impeach your credibility whether or not it is justifiable to do so. Ethically, experts have a responsibility to ensure that their testimony—a product of their scientific and professional judgment—is not misused (see "Ethical Principles of Psychologists," 1992, especially Ethical Standards 1.15 [Misuse of Psychologists' Influence], 1.16 [Misuse of Psychologists' Work], and 7.04 [Truthfulness and Candor]).

Expert witnesses are therefore obliged to become advocates for maintaining the integrity of their opinions. With equal candor, experts must admit to shortcomings and defend their opinions against nonsubstantive attacks (see Public and Professional Communications [VII-D] in "Specialty Guidelines for Forensic Psychologists," 1991). By understanding the adversary process and courtroom communication, experts can help preserve the probity of their testimony.

Courtroom Communications Model

The spirit of the courtroom is captured by Balzac's telling observation that the function of a jury is to decide not the merits of the case but who has the better lawyer. Indeed, it is the responsibility of a court of law to resolve the case before it by listening to attorneys present biased arguments in the most persuasive fashion possible.

It is also important to appreciate that judges and jurors want to be persuaded by expert testimony. Experts take pressure off them by allowing the trier of fact to say, "I made my decision based on the expert's testimony." Experts, however, should never sacrifice truth at the expense of persuasion. Expert witnesses must candidly admit any theoretical, research, or procedural weaknesses in their case conception (Bonnie and Slobogin, 1980).

Although the expert may be genuinely trying to help the court find the truth, his or her impact may depend more on elements of persuasion than on the validity of his or her analyses. Even the most vacuous testimony may be exceptionally persuasive if presented forcefully (Naftulin, Ware, and Donnelly, 1973). Conversely, eminently sound testimony may fall on deaf ears. If participation in a trial is viewed as a de facto exercise in persuasion, then the expert witness must function as an honest and effective communicator by preparing for court realistically (Gutheil and Appelbaum, 1982).

The purpose of the following courtroom communications model is not to endorse attempts at persuasion in court but to acknowledge their existence and identify their processes (Bank, 1986). The model helps expert witnesses become skilled courtroom communicators by applying theory and research from social psychology to courtroom dynamics (Reardon, 1981; Saks and Hastie, 1978).

The expert who is an effective communicator is best able to convey his or her opinion accurately and thus prevent testimony from being distorted during direct examination, cross-examination, and—to a lesser extent—closing arguments. Regardless of the legal issue before the court, the process of testifying persuasively and ethically remains the same (Bank and

Poythress, 1982b). All verbal exchanges in a courtroom can be explained by a communications model with three components: the speaker, the message, and the audience. For our purposes, the speaker is the expert witness, the message is his or her testimony, and the audience is the judge or jury. When any communication occurs, it always does so in a particular setting or background, in this case the courtroom.

Speaker: Source Credibility. To increase persuasiveness, the expert witness must be perceived by the judge or jury as a credible source of information. The concept of credibility has three dimensions: expertise, trustworthiness, and presentational style.

Expertise. Before a witness can be qualified by the trial judge as an expert, he or she must take the stand and present credentials attesting to his or her expertise in the topical area before the court. This includes reviewing academic background, professional training, experience, and other indices of competence. Regarding testimony by experts, Rule 702 of the Federal Rules of Evidence states, "If scientific, technical or other specialized knowledge will assist the trier of fact to understand the evidence or to determine a fact in issue, a witness qualified as an expert by knowledge, skill, experience, training, or education, may testify thereto in the form of an opinion or otherwise."

Attorneys typically elicit such information from experts chronologically. A more effective recitation of qualifications is achieved by presenting credentials categorically. This approach gives the judge and jury a commonsense conceptual framework for defining an expert. The categorical credentialing process has three phases: the attorney conducting *voir dire* explains to the judge and jury that to be considered a mental health expert, the witness must document academic training, experience (applied or research), and familiarity with current advances in the expert's specialization. The witness then meets the three stated requirements for someone to be considered an expert by satisfactorily answering the attorney's categorical questions regarding credentials. The attorney (and judge and jury) can now conclude that the witness is indeed an expert, because he or she has fulfilled the three criteria.

Trustworthiness. Once the judge declares someone an expert, the trustworthiness factor of credibility becomes critical to how the witness's testimony will be received. Doubts concerning the expert's trustworthiness typically stem from the fact that he or she may be privately retained by one litigant, the implication being that the witness is paid to say whatever benefits the party paying the fee. Research demonstrates that testimony from an unbiased source of high expertise will be given more weight than testimony from biased sources with the same perceived expertise (Birnbaum and Stegner, 1979). Unfortunately, even the most objective and honest witness may not be accurately perceived.

Perhaps the most common behavior that undermines an expert's trustworthiness is when he or she changes demeanor, seeming cooperative while responding to direct examination but hostile when coping with cross-examination. Due to anxiety, experts typically become more hesitant while responding during cross-examination. This hesitation can lead judges or jurors to think the expert is trying to be deceptive (Conley, O'Barr, and Lind, 1978).

Experts can avoid contributing to this misperception by presenting the same demeanor while testifying under direct examination and cross-examination. Specifically, if you allow for a short latency of response during direct (even though you may be able to answer immediately), you can then take the same pause while responding under cross without appearing to be more hesitant.

Under direct examination, experts do not want to be misperceived as a yea-sayer or hired gun for the party retaining them. In fact, experts can increase their credibility along the trustworthiness dimension by occasionally disagreeing, when appropriate, with the attorney conducting direct examination. It is also helpful to note that when experts provide opinion testimony, they have the right to say they cannot answer a question because they have not formed an opinion.

Expert witnesses should always be alert to potential ethical problems associated with the expertise and trustworthiness dimensions of source credibility. Regarding expertise, the attorney conducting direct examination may attempt to induce the expert to make exaggerated claims of his or her knowledge or to offer unwarranted criticism of an opposing expert's competence. With reference to trustworthiness, the expert may be encouraged to understate or omit references to procedures or theories that the attorney believes may undermine his or her case. Expert witnesses are, of course, sworn to tell the truth, regardless of how it affects either side.

Presentational Style. This is the most elusive of the three dimensions to credibility. In general, however, it speaks to the issue that the person testifying must behave like an expert in order to convince the judge and jury that he or she is expert.

Experts should dress appropriately, speak clearly and loudly enough for everyone to hear, and avoid appearing defensive even when the cross-examining attorney unloads both barrels. Never forget that the attorney conducting cross-examination is ethically bound to present the best case for his or her client.

Experts are also often advised to stay away from jargon when testifying. This is not necessarily good advice: experts who avoid all jargon may not be meeting the judge's or jury's expectations of how an expert should testify. It is often beneficial to employ some jargon, as long as it is explained in terms that are understandable.

Message: Presenting Effective Testimony. The second component of the courtroom communications model is the speaker's message. For the expert witness, the message is his or her testimony. And as previously mentioned, even the most brilliant analysis may be given little weight if the expert cannot present his or her opinions clearly and convincingly.

Emotional and Logical Appeals. There are two types of persuasive appeal: logical and emotional. Logical appeals invite the trier of fact to reason along with the expert. Emotional appeals utilize poignant language in an attempt to evoke emotions such as sympathy or fear. Logical appeals are aimed at judges or juries in their role as trier of fact, whereas emotional appeals strike a chord with jurors, who sometimes function as the emotional conscience of the community.

The most persuasive experts convey compelling blends of logical and emotional appeals depending on the topic of testimony. Experts, however, are ideally envisioned as objective scientists. If an expert appears too emotionally involved, the judge and jury may think the expert has lost objectivity and give less weight to her or his testimony.

Counterarguments. Perhaps the only constant in court is knowing that one of the two attorneys is going to challenge the expert's case analysis with a rival theory. Under these circumstances—that is, knowing testimony will be rebutted—the negative effects of cross-examination can be mitigated by utilizing the following strategy during direct examination: make a strong appeal for your opinion, identify and explain rival opinions, dismiss them by pointing out their weaknesses, and capitalize on a recency effect by concluding that your opinion is the most valid. This strategy is akin to the medical model's approach to disease prevention—the expert using it effectively inoculates the judge and jury against rival opinions that will be raised by the opposing side.

Audience: Factors Affecting Receptivity to Testimony. The third element of the courtroom communications model concerns the audience's receptivity to testimony. Experts start out with the advantage that most judges and jurors want to be convinced by an expert's testimony because that makes their jobs easier. There are, of course, situations where case facts are overwhelming, thus undercutting the potential influence of expert testimony.

To have any chance of assisting jurors, experts must speak to the level of their audience. The problem with this advice is that most juries include a mix of people with different educational backgrounds, values, and established views on life. Indeed, a jury is best thought of as a collection of individuals rather than a homogeneous group with shared life experiences and values (Bettinghaus, 1973). By nature, juries are ephemeral: they are assembled once for the sole purpose of resolving a legal dispute.

The most effective strategy for reaching the maximum number of jurors is to state opinions in a variety of ways. Wrapping the same content in different verbal packages will likely increase the number of jurors the expert will reach. In metaphorical terms, experts can maximize communication with the greatest number of jurors by coming across, at appropriate times, as a scientist, country doctor, and concerned citizen. Some additional approaches for maintaining jury attention are to utilize voice inflection and eye contact effectively. At critical points in testimony, experts might look jurors straight in the eyes and speak more loudly while delivering crucial details. Perhaps a more direct and effective approach is for experts to simply tell the jurors that what they are about to hear is essential to understanding the case. Never presume that the judge or jury intuits expert testimony. Pivotal details must be explained in order to become part of the court record.

When testimony is concluded, experts should leave the courtroom unless instructed to remain. Experts who voluntarily become part of the gallery or sit by an attorney risk being perceived as overly involved or biased.

Summary

Our democratic principles rest on the belief that truth is discovered through the fair and open combat of ideas in a court of law. When mental health professionals participate in this adversary process as expert witnesses, it is essential for them to understand that attorneys will attempt to impeach their credibility. Mental health professionals who appreciate the spirit and mechanics of courtroom communication will be best prepared to protect the integrity of their testimony.

The courtroom communications model provides experts with a conceptual framework utilizing three components: the speaker is the expert, the message is testimony, and the audience is the judge or jury. Within the structure of this model, communication principles from social psychology can be used to enhance the clarity of testimony and to prevent attorneys from distorting the expert's opinions.

First and foremost, expert witness testimony must be formulated on accepted scholarly and ethical standards. To establish credibility, experts must appear knowledgeable and trustworthy to the judge and jury. The expert must come to court prepared for both direct examination and cross-examination, know when to emphasize logic or emotion, tailor speech in order to reach the maximum number of jurors, and remain nondefensive by projecting the same demeanor regardless of which side is conducting the examination.

The role of the expert witness is forever changing because the judicial system—like the mental health field—continues to evolve. Although the adversary process has undergone dramatic changes over the past eight hundred years, historical vestiges continue to echo throughout our courtrooms.

Today expert witnesses are the champions of both victims and the accused. Legal disputes are increasingly being decided by the battle of the experts, who must undergo the ordeal of cross-examination. When you consider the brutality of ancient ordeals, responding to attorneys armed with questions may not seem so daunting.

References

Bank, S. "Law v. Communication: Persuasive Communication for Attorneys and Experts." *The Champion: Official Journal of the National Association of Criminal Defense Lawyers,* 1986, *10*(9), 19–24.

Bank, S., and Poythress, N. G. "The Elements of Persuasion in Expert Testimony." *Journal of Psychiatry and Law,* Summer 1982a, pp. 173–204.

Bank, S., and Poythress, N. G. "Persuasion and Ethics in Expert Testimony." *Kentucky Defense Counsel Newsletter,* 1982b, 2(2), 2–6.

Bettinghaus, E. *Persuasive Communication.* (2nd ed.) Austin, Tex.: Holt, Rinehart and Winston, 1973.

Birnbaum, M., and Stegner, S. "Source Credibility in Social Judgment: Bias, Expertise, and the Judge's Point of View." *Journal of Personality and Social Psychology,* 1979, 37, 48–74.

Bonnie, R., and Slobogin, C. "The Role of Mental Health Professionals in the Criminal Process: The Case for 'Informed Speculation.'" *Virginia Law Review,* 1980, 66, 427–522.

Brodsky, S. L. "The Mental Health Professional on the Witness Stand: A Survival Guide." In B. Sales (ed.), *Psychology in the Legal Process.* New York: Spectrum, 1977.

Conley, J., O'Barr, W., and Lind, E. "The Power of Language: Presentational Style in the Courtroom." *Duke Law Journal,* 1978, no. 6, pp. 1375–1399.

Eigen, J., and Andoll, G. "From Mad-Doctor to Forensic Witness: The Evolution of Early English Court Psychiatry." *International Journal of Law and Psychiatry,* 1986, 9, 159–169.

"Ethical Principles of Psychologists." *American Psychologist,* 1992, 47(12), 1597–1611.

Faust, D., and Ziskin, J. "The Expert Witness in Psychology and Psychiatry." *Science,* July 1988, 241, 31–35.

Gutheil, T., and Appelbaum, P. *Clinical Handbook of Psychiatry and the Law.* New York: McGraw-Hill, 1982.

Holdsworth, W. *A History of the English Law.* London: Methuen, 1956.

Kempin, F. *Historical Introduction to Anglo-American Law.* (2nd ed.) St. Paul, Minn.: West, 1973.

Naftulin, D., Ware, J., and Donnelly, F. "The Doctor Fox Lecture: A Paradigm of Educational Seduction." *Journal of Medical Education,* 1973, 48, 630–635.

Reardon, K. *Persuasion: Theory and Context.* Thousand Oaks, Calif.: Sage, 1981.

Saks, M. J. "Expert Witness, Nonexpert Witness and Nonwitness Experts," *Law and Human Behavior,* 1990, 14(4), 291–313.

Saks, M. J., and Hastie, R. *Social Psychology in Court.* New York: Van Nostrand Reinhold, 1978.

"Specialty Guidelines for Forensic Psychologists." *Law and Human Behavior,* 1991, 15(6).

Ziskin, J., and Faust, D. *Coping with Psychiatric and Psychological Testimony.* (5th ed.) Los Angeles: Law and Psychology Press, 1995.

STEVEN C. BANK *is assistant to the clinical director at the Center for Forensic Psychiatry in Ann Arbor, Michigan, and past president of the American Board of Forensic Psychology.*

6

This chapter provides an overview of interventions for relatives of severely mentally ill individuals. The author discusses the design and use of these interventions in the context of the cultural characteristics of families and providers, as well as the culture of the interventions themselves.

The Cultural Context of Interventions for Family Members with a Seriously Mentally Ill Relative

Phyllis L. Solomon

A society's beliefs about major psychiatric illness determine how families with an adult relative with a severe mental illness are treated. Cultural belief systems surrounding mental illness influence whether families are informed about the illness, its course, and treatment; whether they are included in the treatment process; and whether providers make any special effort to ease their stress and responsibilities in caring for their relative and managing the illness. This chapter discusses the history and cultural context of the mental health system's beliefs regarding families with a mentally ill relative and the implications of the system's culture for family interventions. It also provides a programmatic definition of family interventions and discusses the implications for the design and use of family interventions of the cultural context of providers, families, and intervention processes and structures. The chapter concludes with an examination of the impact of family interventions on cultural beliefs about adults with severe mental illness and their families, both in the wider society and in the mental health system in particular.

Historical Context of Family Interventions

In the era of asylums, families were considered passive contributors to the onset of mental illness for not having protected their relative from societal disorganization, which was believed to be the principal causal agent (Terkelsen, 1990). Separation from the family was only one element in the process of shielding the patient from the confusion and pressures of the larger society (Terkelsen, 1990). Subsequently, families, particularly parents, were viewed as the causal agents of these disorders. Based on these psychodynamic theories, separation of the ill relative from his or her family persisted, as it was considered essential to helping the patient resolve "issues of parental pathogenesis" (Lefley, 1996, p. 16). As a result of these explanations, families not only were ignored and left uninformed about their relative's diagnosis and treatment but also were blamed for the illness.

Over time, there was a reversal in thinking from complete isolation of the patient from the family as a means of treating the patient to a need to modify the dynamics of the family's interactions. From this conceptualization emerged the need for family therapy to treat the dysfunctional family (Lefley, 1996; Terkelsen, 1990). Families were then put in the position of being confronted with their responsibility for their relative's illness. Psychodynamic and family systems theories about the etiology of major psychiatric illnesses are evident in mental health settings even today (Terkelsen, 1990).

Despite the popularity of these psychogenic theories as explanations for the causes of major psychiatric disorders, their significance waned due to a lack of supporting evidence. Family therapies based on these conceptualizations did not demonstrate clinical benefits (Mueser and Glynn, 1998). Subsequently, there was a shift from belief in a single etiological cause to belief in a combination of biological and environmental factors that result in the onset and course of psychiatric disorders (Coursey, Alford, and Safarjan, 1997; Lehman, Thompson, Dixon, and Scott, 1995). These biopsychosocial explanatory models of vulnerability or stress diathesis inspired comprehensive treatment programs consisting of medication for patients and psychosocial treatment for their families.

The development of psychosocial interventions for families of adults with severe mental illness was stimulated by research that found that recently released patients who returned to families who were highly critical, overinvolved, and hostile or labeled as high in expressed emotion (EE) were more likely to relapse than those who returned to low-EE families (Mueser and Glynn, 1998; Vaughn and Leff, 1976; Brown, Birley, and Wing, 1972). These findings precipitated a host of investigations of randomized controlled trials of family interventions to change the family environment and reduce patient relapse (Dixon and Lehman, 1995; Lam, 1991; Strachan, 1986; Hogarty, Anderson, and Reiss, 1987). There is much controversy surrounding this research, however, as it continues to blame families, and the direction of causality of high EE is unclear (Hatfield, Spaniol, and Zipple, 1987; Mintz, Liberman, Miklowitz, and Mintz, 1987).

In an independent effort, families who were dissatisfied with the treatment provided to their relative, the lack of communication between them and their family member's mental health care providers, and provider attitudes toward families came together in various locales across the country to form support and advocacy groups (Shetler, 1986). The exponential growth in these groups was undoubtedly stimulated by deinstitutionalization, which left the care of ill relatives largely up to their families. The social stigma associated with mental illness resulted in isolation of families, who feared the repercussions of disclosing their relative's illness to others. These families met to share experiences and find support. Individuals from these grassroots support groups met in 1979 in Madison, Wisconsin, to form a national coalition of these independent groups, the National Alliance for the Mentally Ill (NAMI) (Shetler, 1986). NAMI not only advocates for legislative changes but also has been the impetus for an enormous expansion of local support groups.

Defining Family Interventions

The emergence of family interventions reflects a shift from viewing families as the cause of mental illness to viewing them as a resource and a source of support for their ill relative (Marsh and Johnson, 1997). To some extent, this shift was necessitated by the deinstitutionalization movement, which as noted previously left families the de facto caregivers for their ill relatives, a role for which they had no training or knowledge and that often brought enormous stress and burdens. A family intervention in such cases can be defined as any strategy or program, clinical or nonclinical, designed to help and empower these families to cope with these devastating disorders through such means as the provision of support, education, and skill training. Family interventions may be provided by professionals or nonprofessionals, including family members themselves. Diverse interventions meet this definition, including psychoeducation, family education, family consultation, family support and advocacy groups, and other forms of assistance to families, including marital and family therapy and respite care. Although only psychoeducation has been extensively researched, all of these interventions are generally perceived as helpful by family members, as they serve different functions.

Types of Family Interventions

There is a diverse array of family interventions that are clinical as well as nonclinical. The following discussion provides an overview of these interventions.

Psychoeducation. Psychoeducation models are typically a component of a comprehensive treatment program for the ill relative (Solomon, 1996). Most interventions draw on social learning, behavioral theory, and cognitive theory. If relevant, they may focus on reduction of high EE, although interventions are needed by low-EE families as well. All psychoeducational models include "education about the illness, support for families, problem-solving strategies, and illness management techniques" (Lefley, 1996, p. 132). For some interventions, the ill relative is present; others include separate sessions for the ill family member. All are designed, delivered, and evaluated by professionals (sometimes a team of professionals). Many are delivered in clinical settings, but some are delivered in the family's home. These interventions usually require a relatively long-term commitment on the part of the family, anywhere from nine months to two years or more. They are often initiated at a crisis point for the family, such as during hospitalization or upon discharge. The educational component may be an initial step toward entering traditional family therapy. For the most part, these interventions have been research efforts. In most mental health systems, they have not become a part of routine treatment, although their efficacy has been demonstrated (Dixon and Lehman, 1995).

Family Consultation (Supportive Family Counseling). Family consultation is often provided by a professional but sometimes by a trained family member. The consultant offers expert advice and information either to an individual family member or to the whole family unit (Bernheim, 1982; Bernheim and Lehman, 1985; Kanter, 1985). This is a flexible and collaborative approach to working with families (Marsh and Johnson, 1997). As adapted by the Training and Education Center (TEC) Network of Philadelphia, this intervention has three phases. In the first phase, of feeling or connecting, the consultant takes a brief history of the relative's illness, offers empathy and support, acknowledges family strengths, addresses issues of guilt and blame, and assesses the family's need for education and skill development. In the next, or focusing, phase, the consultant develops an agenda for the family's educational program, clarifies its problems, and creates a prioritized list of objectives. In the final, or finding, phase, the consultant helps the family develop strategies for meeting the agreed-upon objectives. Besides helping family members develop new skills, the consultant might also evaluate their use of those skills in relating to the ill relative, inform them about appropriate community resources, and occasionally accompany them to meetings with service agencies (Mannion, Meisel, Draine, and Solomon, 1997). TEC provides some of these services by phone, and recently it adapted this model to a group format (Mannion, Meisel, Draine, and Solomon, 1997). The structure and process of TEC's group format intervention is similar to the multifamily approach, except that the ill family member is not included in the TEC model (McFarlane and others, 1995).

Family Education. Family education is a nonclinical intervention that has a strengths approach as its theoretical base, with stress reduction, improved coping, and adaptation as its targeted outcomes. In contrast to psychoeducation, which was designed to meet the needs of the ill relative, family education was developed primarily to meet the needs of families. These programs come from an adult-learning and health promotion orientation. Family education does not presume any family dysfunction, as does the more medical emphasis of some psychoeducational models. Goals of this intervention are to increase the family's knowledge of the disorder, increase their coping skills, alleviate their burden and stress, and improve quality of life for them and their ill relative (Hatfield, 1994; Solomon, 1996). Family education is generally implemented in a group format, with didactic lectures the primary format, perhaps supplemented with audio or visual aids. Frequently, these interventions also include experiential elements, offering participants the opportunity to practice the skills being taught. They are usually short-term interventions, consisting of anywhere from a couple of hours in a single day to multiple two- or three-hour sessions over a ten- or twelve-week period. These interventions have been developed and delivered by professionals, by family members, and by a combination of the two. Generally, the ill relative is not a participant, so families can be comfortable in discussing their concerns. The group format offers support, empathy, and a chance to share experiences. Many such interventions arise from freestanding grassroots efforts; others are part of mental health programs. The research on these programs is very limited, but they show promise in terms of achieving their goals (Solomon, 1996; Solomon, Draine, Mannion, and Meisel, 1996, 1997). The most noted family education program, currently offered in numerous communities nationwide, is NAMI's Family-to-Family program (formerly called the Journey of Hope).

Family Support and Advocacy Groups. Family support groups are an essential nonclinical intervention for families of adults with severe mental illness (Lefley, 1996). They provide support, information, understanding, and opportunities to pursue advocacy (Marsh and Johnson, 1997). Member-facilitated group sessions offer contact with others who have shared similar experiences. Members share resources, information, coping strategies, and ideas for managing their ill relative (Lefley, 1996). Frequently, these groups sponsor lectures and educational programs. Families often want more from these groups than simply a forum for sharing their grief and pain. They want to move toward action. Specifically, members want "to eradicate mental illness, to change the system, to provide needed services, to fight stigma, to obtain a better quality of life for their loved ones" (Lefley, 1996, p. 141). Advocacy gives purpose and meaning to the lives of these families and becomes a therapeutic tool for them. These families therefore advocate for a variety of policy and legislative changes at both the local and national levels.

Other Interventions. There are also other, more specialized interventions, such as one for children of parents with serious affective disorders (Lefley, 1996). There are financial-planning programs for parents wondering how to provide for the future of an ill adult child and respite care, which offers families relief from the stresses of caregiving. In some instances, there may be a need to develop interventions in response to specific issues. For example, in certain situations families resort to the use of restraining orders (Solomon, Draine, and Delaney, 1995); a mediation intervention may be effective in such cases to prevent the need for future restraining orders.

The family interventions discussed here are generally educational and supportive, serving the family's needs for information, skill acquisition, and emotional support. When these services are not sufficient, individual, family, and marital therapy are also available (Marsh and Johnson, 1997). Although these types of interventions might not help a family relate to their ill relative, they can help family members deal with personal problems resulting from or exacerbated by having a relative with severe mental illness (Lefley, 1996; Marsh and Johnson, 1997).

In addition, family interventions can be incorporated into other services, such as case management (Solomon, Draine, Mannion, and Meisel, 1997). For example, multifamily group therapy has been integrated into an assertive community treatment (ACT) case management program, Family-Aided Assertive Community Treatment (FACT); integrating a crisis family intervention into an ACT program is another alternative (McFarlane and others, 1996). McFarlane and his colleagues note that inclusion of the family in the treatment process differed from the orientation of the original program model, which emphasized "constructive separation" of the client from the family. This separation was based on the premise that crisis resolution would be hindered if the ill relative interacted with his or her family (1996).

The Impact of Family Culture

Ethnicity is a major determinant of people's belief systems. It influences families' beliefs about what causes mental illness and their attitudes toward mental health care providers. A family's ethnicity also has an impact on which interventions are likely to resolve their problems related to a family member's disorder. Furthermore, the definition of what constitutes a family differs by cultural groups (McGoldrick, 1982), as do the roles different family members assume within the family context. These factors in turn affect families' behaviors during mental health interventions and the types of interventions they are willing to pursue. Certain ethnic groups, particularly African Americans and other minority groups, have not participated in family interventions to any great extent. This has been the situation with clinical interventions, such as psychoeducation, as well as with nonclinical ones, such as family education and support groups. This has also been the situation in research on these interventions and other related issues, such as burden and caregiving relief. As a consequence, the effectiveness of these interventions for minority groups is unclear.

For family interventions to be attractive to the diverse array of families with a relative with severe mental illness, they must be sensitive to cultural variations. Deciding whether interventions should be designed by families, by professionals, or jointly requires a consideration of a variety of family cultures, as cultural issues influence the "accessibility and acceptability" of mental health services (Guarnaccia and Parra, 1996). In addition, some approaches may not be sufficient for certain groups. For example, Lefley

(1990) indicates that structured family therapy, which helps restore traditional family relationships, may be more beneficial than psychoeducation for immigrant groups in which role changes are eroding the established family structure. Jordan, Lewellen, and Vandiver (1995) delineate particular considerations and recommendations for family education programs for Laotian, African American, and Mexican American families.

One factor of importance to be considered in the design of such programs is the cultural definition of a family. For example, in some cultures the family may go beyond the nuclear family to the extended family. It may also be important for members of some cultural groups to include folk healers, priests, and other nonblood members, such as godparents, in family interventions (Jordan, Lewellen, and Vandiver, 1995). Sharing problems with strangers may be inherently antithetical to some groups' values. In these situations, a family consultation model may be more appropriate than a group approach. Cultural sensitivity on the part of the provider is crucial in making appropriate referrals, modifying existing interventions, and developing new ones. Providers may be inaccurate in assuming a family needs a particular intervention. The family may need the information or support that a particular intervention can provide, but this does not necessarily mean they need that intervention, as another may be culturally more suitable.

Also, families from some cultures may not feel a need for emotional support from strangers, as they have an extended support system consisting of friends and their church. Research by Pickett, Vraniak, Cook, and Cohler (1993) found that black families accommodate and adjust to an ill child more readily than white families. The explanation these investigators put forth was that blacks may not hold "normative-development expectations regarding age-appropriate behavior" to the same extent as white families (p. 465). Some cultures do not find the term mental illness acceptable, and other cultures may find it disrespectful to set limits on older family members. Consequently, different terminology and program structures may be necessary for particular cultural groups (Lundwall, 1996). It remains an open question whether effective groups need to be culturally homogeneous (Shankar, 1994); however, maintaining group homogeneity may be essential to attract families from a particular culture and ensure their comfort with the process.

For the most part, all of these interventions, both the clinical and the nonclinical ones, are designed for parents with an adult child with severe mental illness (mainly schizophrenia). Because people with psychiatric illness now spend the majority of their time in the community and are having children of their own, these interventions require modifications. Family members with different relationships to the mentally ill individual have different role interactions and responsibilities and therefore need different information and support. Mannion, Mueser, and Solomon (1994) point out the importance of specifically designing programs for spouses of someone with a severe mental illness. Frequently, when spouses do attend a local NAMI meeting, they do not stay long enough to get involved or to realize that other spouses do occasionally show up (Mannion, Mueser, and Solomon, 1994; Mannion, 1996). The needs of siblings of mentally ill individuals have often been overlooked in educational and support interventions (Lundwall, 1996). Likewise, adult children of mentally ill individuals have been neglected by family education efforts, and interventions for younger children require still more modification.

The Impact of Professional Culture

Clinicians' attitudes toward families are a product of their clinical training (Lefley, 1990). Due to a variety of factors, including recent research, negative views regarding the role families play in the etiology and management of their relatives' illness have changed; nevertheless, some mental health professionals continue to reject and ignore families (Lefley, 1988, 1996). This results from the fact that some of those who were trained during an earlier time continue to practice and teach without updating themselves on current research. Furthermore, training programs are a reflection of the values, theories, and research interests of their institutional faculty and administrations (Lefley, 1990). One family therapist who works effectively with families of adults with severe mental illness frequently comments that she is a "recovering" family therapist; in other words, she is recovering from her training in the area of working with families of persons with a severe mental illness. Inevitably, the professional and personal values of practitioners, including their own cultural socialization, influence the design of any program they develop. Similarly, these same values also play a role in the information they provide about these interventions and in which patients they refer to them. For example, practitioners can use confidentiality issues to justify not working with families, rather than attempting to resolve this professional conflict (see Marsh and Johnson, 1997, for ways to resolve potential confidentiality problems in working with families). There are a number of opportunities for practitioners to update themselves on recent developments in family interventions and family research, should their values move them in this direction.

Cultural Aspects of the Design and Use of Interventions

Interventions, too, have cultures, insofar as the participants share attitudes, values, goals, and practices. For individual interventions, the practitioner's and family members' engagement and their commitment to forming an alliance affect the rates of retention and the benefits of the intervention to the family. The degree of alliance is contingent on shared beliefs and goals between the family and the practitioner. In addition, whether the intervention is delivered in the home, a clinic, or another setting, as well as the auspices under which it is offered, affect the culture of the intervention and thus its attractiveness to families and rate of retention. The availability and accessibility of the intervention are also crucial to its attractiveness to families. For some families, home-delivered or over-the-phone interventions are far more attractive and comfortable. Budd and Hughes (1997) found that one of the most helpful aspects of family interventions was families' knowing that they could contact the practitioner for help and advice should problems or difficulties arise.

The factors that influence group interventions' cultures are somewhat more complicated. Factors such as group size, participation of the ill relative, setting, administrative auspices, degree of homogeneity of the membership, and whether the group is led by a professional or by a family member affect the intervention's attractiveness and the retention of family members. Hatfield (1997) noted that NAMI members are raising questions with regard to which characteristics are appropriate for sorting participants of support groups. Participants of support groups are frequently diverse with regard to "age of caregiver and ill relative, length of illness, caregiver relationship to ill member, diagnoses, ethnicity, and other characteristics" (p. 259). Leaders feel that groups should be more homogeneous for participants to optimally benefit, but as of yet there has been no research regarding which group member characteristics need to be the same. These issues are relevant not only for support groups but also for educational and therapy groups.

The length of time a group has been in existence and the degree of turnover in the group also affect the intervention's culture. Families are initially attracted to support groups to meet their needs for information and support, but as these needs are met, members tend to move toward a desire for advocacy. When families with a recently diagnosed relative attend a local support group that focuses on advocacy, they frequently do not return after their initial meeting (Citron, Solomon, and Draine, 1999). Some groups now recognize this evolutionary change toward advocacy in intervention cultures and designate a particular member to spend time with new attendees. This is a potential solution to the problem of retaining new members, as it offers new participants an opportunity to develop a relationship with the group by having someone to listen to their concerns and share experiences with.

The Feedback Loop: The Impact of Family Interventions on Stigma and Views About Families

As family interventions for adults with severe mental illness have exponentially increased, these interventions have had an impact on society's view of adults with severe mental illness and their families. For example, the advocacy efforts of NAMI and its local affiliates, directed at educating the public in general and federal and state legislators in particular, have improved people's understanding of mental illness as a brain disease and have resulted in increased empathy for families. Similarly, NAMI's antistigma campaign has made the public more aware of some of the myths and inaccuracies surrounding mental illness that have been perpetuated by the media.

These interventions also offer families increased understanding of their ill relative's disorders and greater confidence in their ability to assertively voice their and their relative's needs to providers in the mental health system. Families that are well-informed, articulate, and willing to communicate essential information regarding their relative's symptoms and behaviors contribute much to changing provider attitudes. Consequently, interventions that educate families have the potential to improve the mental health system, both for individuals with mental illness and for their families. With a receptive attitude toward families, providers can learn much from collaborating with them, in terms of developing the most beneficial interventions for patients and in terms of planning services and strategies for working with family members. Even without highly structured interventions for families, family-provider collaboration serves the best interests of everyone. For too long, the mental health system has either ignored or blamed the family. Frequently, when family members are considered, it is only in the context of what they can provide their ill relative, whether it be housing or financial or emotional support. If family members are assessed as needing help themselves, they are typically referred to existing services or treatments, such as family or marital therapy, rather than offered interventions responsive to their specific needs and desires.

It is hoped that this chapter has achieved its purpose of spreading the message that family interventions are quite varied and consequently have value for a wide array of families. Furthermore, most families can benefit from education, support, and training in coping and management strategies. However, for the greatest number of families to benefit from such interventions, the cultural context of the families and of the interventions themselves needs to be taken into consideration, both in the design and development of the interventions and in referral practices. Providers cannot continue to adopt a procrustean approach to meeting the needs of families with a relative with severe mental illness. There is a plethora of helpful family interventions that can be adapted from the existing array of models. The one-size-fits-all approach will not best serve the diversity of families affected by a relative with a severe psychiatric disorder.

References

Bernheim, K. F. "Supportive Family Counseling." *Schizophrenia Bulletin*, 1982, *8*, 634–640.
Bernheim, K. F., and Lehman, A. F. *Working with Families of the Mentally Ill*. New York: Norton, 1985.
Brown, G., Birley, J., and Wing, J. "Influence of Psychiatric Illness." *British Journal of Psychiatry*, 1972, *121*, 241–258.

Budd, R., and Hughes, I. "What Do Relatives of People with Schizophrenia Find Helpful About Family Intervention?" *Schizophrenia Bulletin*, 1997, *23*, 341–347.

Citron, M., Solomon, P., and Draine, J. "Self-Help Groups for Families of Persons with Mental Illness: Perceived Benefits of Helpfulness." *Community Mental Health Journal*, 1999, *35*, 15–30.

Coursey, R., Alford, J., and Safarjan, B. "Significant Advances in Understanding and Treating Serious Mental Illness." *Professional Psychology: Research and Practice*, 1997, *28*, 205–216.

Dixon, L., and Lehman, A. "Family Interventions for Schizophrenia." *Schizophrenia Bulletin*, 1995, *21*, 631–643.

Guarnaccia, P., and Parra, P. "Ethnicity, Social Status, and Families' Experiences of Caring for a Mentally Ill Family Member." *Community Mental Health Journal*, 1996, *32*, 243–260.

Hatfield, A. B. "Family Education: Theory and Practice." In A. B. Hatfield (ed.), *Family Interventions in Mental Illness*. New Directions for Mental Health Services, no. 62. San Francisco: Jossey-Bass, 1994.

Hatfield, A. B. "Families of Adults with Severe Mental Illness: New Directions for Research." *American Journal of Orthopsychiatry*, 1997, *67*, 254–260.

Hatfield, A. B., Spaniol, L., and Zipple, A. "Expressed Emotion: A Family Perspective." *Schizophrenia Bulletin*, 1987, *13*, 221–226.

Hogarty, G. E., Anderson, C. M., and Reiss, D. J. "Family Psychoeducation, Social Skills Training, and Medication in Schizophrenia: The Long and Short of It." *Psychopharmacology Bulletin*, 1987, *23*, 12–13.

Jordan, C., Lewellen, A., and Vandiver, V. "Psychoeducation for Minority Families: A Social Work Perspective." *International Journal of Mental Health*, 1995, *23*(4), 27–43.

Kanter, J. "Consulting with Families of the Chronic Mentally Ill." In J. Kanter (ed.), *Clinical Issues in Treating the Chronic Mentally Ill*. New Directions for Mental Health Services, no. 27. San Francisco: Jossey-Bass, 1985.

Lam, D. "Psychosocial Family Interventions in Schizophrenia: A Review of Empirical Studies." *Psychological Medicine*, 1991, *21*, 423–441.

Lefley, H. "Training Professionals to Work with Families of Chronic Patients." *Community Mental Health Journal*, 1988, *24*, 338–357.

Lefley, H. "Cultural Issues in Training Psychiatric Residents to Work with Families of the Long-Term Mentally Ill." In E. Sorel (ed.), *Family, Culture and Psychobiology*. New York: Legas, 1990.

Lefley, H. *Family Caregiving in Mental Illness*. Thousand Oaks, Calif.: Sage, 1996.

Lehman, A., Thompson, J., Dixon, L., and Scott, J. "Schizophrenia: Treatment Outcomes Research." *Schizophrenia Bulletin*, 1995, *21*, 561–566.

Lundwall, R. "How Psychoeducation Support Groups Can Provide Multidiscipline Services to Families of People with Mental Illness." *Psychiatric Rehabilitation Journal*, 1996, *20*, 64–71.

Mannion, E. "Resilience and Burden in Spouses of People with Mental Illness." *Psychiatric Rehabilitation Journal*, 1996, *20*, 13–23.

Mannion, E., Meisel, M., Draine, J., and Solomon, P. "Applying Research on Family Education About Mental Illness to Development of a Relative's Group Consultation Model." *Community Mental Health Journal*, 1997, *33*, 555–569.

Mannion, E., Mueser, K., and Solomon, P. "Designing Psychoeducational Services for Spouses of Persons with Serious Mental Illness." *Community Mental Health Journal*, 1994, *30*, 177–190.

Marsh, D., and Johnson, D. L. "The Family Experience of Mental Illness: Implications for Interventions." *Professional Psychology: Research and Practice*, 1997, *28*, 229–237.

McFarlane, W., and others. "Psychoeducational Multiple Family Groups: Four-Year Relapse Outcome in Schizophrenia." *Family Process*, 1995, *34*, 127–144.

McFarlane, W., and others. "A Comparison of Two Levels of Family-Aided Assertive Community Treatment." *Psychiatric Services*, 1996, *47*, 744–750.

McGoldrick, M. "Ethnicity and Family Therapy: An Overview." In M. McGoldrick, J. Pearce, and J. Giordano (eds.), *Ethnicity and Family Therapy*. New York: Guilford Press, 1982.

Mintz, L., Liberman, R., Miklowitz, D., and Mintz, J. "Expressed Emotion: A Call for Partnership Among Relatives, Patients, and Professionals." *Schizophrenia Bulletin*, 1987, 13, 227–235.

Mueser, K., and Glynn, S. "Family Intervention for Schizophrenia." In K. S. Dobson and K. D. Craig (eds.), *Best Practice: Developing and Promoting Empirically Validated Interventions*. Thousand Oaks, Calif.: Sage, 1998.

Pickett, S., Vraniak, D., Cook, J., and Cohler, B. "Strength in Adversity: Blacks Bear Burden Better Than Whites." *Professional Psychology: Research and Practice*, 1993, 24, 460–467.

Shankar, R. "Interventions with Families of People with Schizophrenia in India." In A.B. Hatfield (ed.), *Family Interventions in Mental Illness*. New Directions for Mental Health Services, no. 62. San Francisco: Jossey-Bass, 1994.

Shetler, H. *A History of the National Alliance for the Mentally Ill*. Arlington, Va.: National Alliance for the Mentally Ill, 1986.

Solomon, P. "Moving from Psychoeducation to Family Education for Families of Adults with Serious Mental Illness." *Psychiatric Services*, 1996, 47, 1364–1370.

Solomon, P., Draine, J., and Delaney, M. "The Use of Restraining Orders by Families of Severely Mentally Ill Adults." *Administration and Policy in Mental Health*, 1995, 23, 157–161.

Solomon, P., Draine, J., Mannion, E., and Meisel, M. "Impact of Brief Family Psychoeducation on Self-Efficacy." *Schizophrenia Bulletin*, 1996, 22, 41–50.

Solomon, P., Draine, J., Mannion, E., and Meisel, M. "Effectiveness of Two Models of Brief Family Education: Retention of Gains by Family Members of Adults with Serious Mental Illness." *American Journal of Orthopsychiatry*, 1997, 67, 177–186.

Strachan, A. "Family Intervention for the Rehabilitation of Schizophrenia: Toward Protection and Coping." *Schizophrenia Bulletin*, 1986, 12, 678–698.

Terkelsen, K. "A Historical Perspective on Family-Provider Relationships." In H. P. Lefley and D. L. Johnson (eds.), *Families as Allies in the Treatment of the Mentally Ill*. Washington, D.C.: American Psychiatric Press, 1990.

Vaughn, C., and Leff, J. "The Influence of Family and Social Factors on the Course of Psychiatric Illness." *British Journal of Psychiatry*, 1976, 129, 125–137.

PHYLLIS L. SOLOMON is professor at the University of Pennsylvania School of Social Work and professor of social work in psychiatry at the University of Pennsylvania School of Medicine.

7

Mental health professionals have raised concerns about the role of spirituality and religion in services for people with severe mental disorders, but this chapter offers compelling reasons for increased attention to spiritual issues in service delivery.

The Place of Spirituality and Religion in Mental Health Services

Roger D. Fallot

There is a long history of mutual skepticism, if not antagonism, in the relationship between science and religion. As mental health practice became increasingly allied with natural science and rationalistic paradigms in the early twentieth century, many psychiatrists and psychologists wrote dismissively of spiritual or religious experience. Freud's (1927) characterization of religion as illusion and his analogy between religious ritual and obsessive-compulsive behaviors (1913) have come to represent a central fear of many spiritually committed people: that mental health professionals at best reduce religious conviction and practice to psychological processes and at worst actively derogate spirituality in its entirety.

Conversely, some religious people have adamantly denied the value of secular mental health services. Sharing the assumption of an inherent and irreducible conflict between scientific and religious worldviews, these individuals have counseled people to rely solely on religious sources of help for mental disorders and problems in living. Like the psychologists who reject a significant place for religion, these religionists reject a significant role for the human sciences.

In addition to the more extreme positions of mutual rejection, however, have been numerous attempts to find collaborative and integrative models for psychology and religion—models for theory, practice, and professional organization (see Vande Kemp, 1996, and Wulff, 1996, for helpful overviews of these diverse movements). Especially in the past twenty years, the value of constructive relations, both mutually supportive and mutually critical, between the behavioral and medical sciences on the one hand and between religion and spirituality on the other has become evident in the literature of both disciplines (for example, Browning, 1987; Shafranske, 1996a). Psychiatry's increased openness to recognizing the import of religion in clients' lives is evidenced in the DSM-IV inclusion of religious or spiritual problems as potentially appropriate foci of clinical attention (DSM-IV, 1994; Lukoff, Lu, and Turner, 1992). A committee recently developed and presented to the American Psychiatric Association a model curriculum for training psychiatric residents in religious issues. Several book-length reviews have summarized and evaluated the literature relating religion to mental health or to clinical practice (Schumaker, 1992; Shafranske, 1996a; Pargament, 1997a; Koenig, 1998).

Despite this increased interest, however, little has been written about the place of religion and spirituality in the lives of people with severe mental illnesses. The first purpose of this chapter is to explore some of the concerns that have led to this relative neglect of spirituality in relation to serious mental illness, defined as schizophrenia, major depression, and bipolar and schizoaffective disorders. The second goal is to outline, by way of contrast, some of the clinical, theoretical, and empirical reasons for giving increased attention to spirituality in services for this population.

Definitional Issues

Definitions of *spirituality* and *religion* in both the clinical and research literatures have often been confusing and ambiguous. Attempts to refine these concepts for research purposes are ongoing (Zinnbauer and others, 1997). For some authors, religion is the more encompassing of the two constructs. Pargament (1997a), for example, sees religion as "the search for significance in ways related to the sacred" (p. 32), whereas spirituality refers to religion's most central function—the "search for the sacred" (p. 39).

For other writers, spirituality is the larger of the two concepts (Koenig, 1994) and may or may not include religion. The general approach among this group is to identify religion more or less closely with its institutional base. Religiousness, for instance, can refer to "adherence to the beliefs and practices of an organized church or religious institution" (Shafranske and Malony, 1990, p. 72). Spirituality, in this view, has primarily personal and experiential connotations. It may refer to a broad-based search for meaning and belonging in connection with core values (Sperry and Giblin, 1996) or to a relationship with a transcendent realm or being. From this perspective, personal spirituality may find expression in organized religious contexts, or it may remain outside these communities.

Because the ambiguities and multivalent meanings in these concepts are not likely to be resolved in the near future, it is important to be clear about each author's understanding and use of the terms. I will adopt a convention that emphasizes *experiential* and *institutional* dimensions. Experientially, both spirituality and religion may involve the following: a sense of ultimate meaning, a purpose, and values; a relationship with a transcendent being or higher power; or a sense of the sacred or holy. In this way, one core traditional meaning of *religion* is virtually synonymous with *spirituality*. By that definition, a religious experience would not differ much conceptually from a spiritual experience.

An additional meaning of religion, though, is also necessary and refers to its institutional context. Here, religion may entail a defined set of beliefs (a doctrine), rituals, and practice, as well as an identifiable community of believers. Spirituality may also find group expression, but to the extent that group spiritual experience becomes formalized, it moves toward meeting the criteria for institutional religion.

Pargament (1997b) makes a compelling case for avoiding the dichotomy of good personal spirituality and bad institutional religion—an implicit bias in some models. The convention adopted in this chapter assumes no differential valuation of spirituality and religion. It further assumes that spirituality and religion both have personal, experiential dimensions and may have, to varying degrees of formal organization, communal expressions. When I wish to emphasize more formal religion as opposed to spiritual or religious experience, I will refer to it as organized or institutional religion.

Contextual Issues

Sociologists and historians of religion have pointed out the high level of religious involvement that characterizes the people of the United States. According to Finke and Stark (1992), there has been a gradual increase in participation in organized religion from the colonial period into the twentieth century, with current levels of religious adherence reaching nearly two-thirds of the population. Although specific religious groups and denominations have shifted markedly in size, the overall trend has been one of consistent growth. Immigration has added to the already tremendous range of Judeo-Christian expressions by bringing, among others, large and diverse numbers of Hindus, Muslims, Sikhs, and Buddhists.

Not only is there broad involvement in institutional religion in this country but there is a correspondingly prevalent set of beliefs about religion and its importance in daily life. Over 90 percent of the U.S. population say they believe in God, and nearly 90 percent report that they pray—the majority doing so daily (Gallup and Castelli, 1989; Hastings and Hastings, 1996). Measures of religious commitment might yield even stronger findings if a less institutional and traditional set of criteria were adopted—for example, if people who identified themselves as spiritual but not religious were included as well (Zinnbauer and others, 1997). In this broader social and cultural context, the relative inattention to matters of religion and spirituality in mental health programming is striking indeed. And given the movement of the past two decades toward more inclusive, multidimensional (holistic) assessments and the similarly comprehensive and integrated service arrangements in community-based treatment, the lack of attention to spirituality in the lives of mental health service consumers is all the more noteworthy.

Concerns About Religion and Spirituality in Mental Health Services

A wide variety of beliefs has limited the ways in which religion and spirituality might be addressed in services for people with severe mental disorders. A review of some of these factors is important to understanding the theoretical, clinical, and personal convictions that result in minimizing or avoiding religious issues.

First, as noted earlier, is the historical antagonism between the biobehavioral sciences and religion. In certain psychodynamic and cognitive-rational traditions, for example, religion is closely tied to maladaptive defensive functions, to irrational and distorted views of reality, or to automatically rigid and dogmatic patterns of thinking. On such theoretical grounds, some mental health professionals interpret religious experience as inherently regressive, primitive, or dysfunctional. Such concerns are often heightened in working with people who have severe mental illnesses and for whom delusions and hallucinations are not uncommon. In these cases, the clinician may have difficulty—both conceptually and clinically—in distinguishing, for example, between religious delusions and valid commitments.

Premature judgments rooted in a theoretical connection between religion and psychopathology fail to do justice to the multiple and diverse functions that religious and spiritual experience may play in the lives of consumers (see, for example, Sullivan, 1993). Literature that is both clinical and theoretical (for example, Meissner, 1984), as well as the research literature (Gartner, 1996; Schumaker, 1992), has demonstrated the complexity of the relationship between religion and psychosocial functioning. Before arriving at a conclusion about a consumer's religious or spiritual experience, clinicians need to make a careful assessment of the role of that experience in the consumer's overall life structure and functioning.

These difficulties in sorting through thorny questions of reality and illusion are related to a second concern raised by clinicians. For many professionals, addressing religion or spirituality is potentially disorganizing for people who may have (or have had at one time) delusional thoughts with religious content. And it may be confusing and counterproductive for many others because religious language is so often abstract, metaphorical, and symbolic. If one of the central cognitive deficits in the schizophrenic spectrum disorders is a failure to maintain adequate distance or to make necessary distinctions between the immediate and the abstract, this argument goes, then such discussions may undermine a more helpful focus on the concrete necessities of daily life.

Although it is certainly plausible that using language too closely allied with delusional thinking may lead to a strengthening of such content, there is little reason to single out religious language in this regard. Clearly, the clinical adoption of *any* language needs to be weighed in terms of its impact on, and relationship to, the consumer's beliefs and perceptions. In addition, it is probable that such concern with entrenching delusional processes is overdrawn. People with severe mental illnesses are rarely talked into, or out of, delusional beliefs. In fact, the sensitive exploration of these convictions may yield a great deal of important information for assessment and service planning (Fitchett, Burton, and Sivan, 1997). Again, appropriate concern with the process of such discussions is not addressed adequately by avoiding them altogether.

Similarly, the idea that using religious abstractions distracts people with severe mental disorders from daily realities rests on two questionable assumptions: (1) that it is possible to avoid such abstract language and (2) that religious abstractions automatically compete with concrete realities. Much language—religious and nonreligious—is metaphorical in nature; it is simply impossible to avoid analogies, metaphors, and abstractions in usual conversation. For clinicians, the key is to understand the impact a particular set of metaphors, symbols, or abstractions is likely to have on work with a particular consumer. Second, clinical interviews, psychotherapy experiences, and ongoing group discussions indicate that most individuals with mental illness (when not acutely, severely psychotic) are not disorganized by exploring religious experience nor are they less able to attend to concrete daily tasks as a result of such exploration. For some individuals, in fact, having religious language available to them serves as a reinforcement for concentration on specific day-to-day challenges in areas such as substance abuse and trauma recovery (Fallot, 1997). Again, the clinical challenge is to understand the function of religious or spiritual language in the consumer's life rather than to reject such language on overgeneralized grounds.

A third factor in the relative neglect of religious and spiritual dimensions of consumers' lives may be the so-called religiosity gap between mental health professionals and the general public (Lukoff, Lu, and Turner, 1992). Organized religion and certain traditional religious beliefs apparently play a smaller role in the lives of psychologists and psychiatrists than in other people's lives. These mental health professionals tend to be notably less involved in institutional religion, less likely to believe in the existence of God, and less likely to see religion as important than the population as a whole (Lukoff, Lu, and Turner, 1992; Ragan, Malony, and Beit-Hallahmi, 1980; Shafranske, 1996b). Such findings are consistent with other large-scale surveys showing that with more education and higher occupational prestige, a "privatization" of religion and diminished involvement with conventional religiosity is more likely (Greer and Roof, 1992).

Although psychologists as a group thus differ from the general public in religious affiliation, participation, and particular beliefs, they are not especially negative about religion's overall role in human life. The majority of respondents in one survey of psychologists found that 53 percent saw religion as valuable, whereas only 14 percent considered it undesirable (Shafranske and Malony, 1990, p. 73). The relative lack of personal commitment to religion does not seem to generalize, then, to psychologists' views of religion as a dimension of people's experience. This may be partly due to the value psychologists place on *spirituality*; they consider it more personally relevant and generally salient than religion (Shafranske, 1996b). There does not appear to be a spirituality gap that is comparable to the gap in religious affiliation and belief (Lukoff, Lu, and Turner, 1992). In fact, one recent study found that, next to participants in New Age groups, mental health workers were most likely (44 percent) to identify themselves as "spiritual but not religious" (Zinnbauer and others, 1997). This differential commitment to spirituality may have two distinct implications. On the positive side, it may serve to enhance clinicians' acceptance of the varieties of religious and spiritual experience. On the negative side, to the extent that clinicians see themselves as valuing spirituality over religion, they may explicitly or implicitly communicate a negative bias toward organized religion in their clinical work.

In exploring the roles religion and spirituality may play in the lives of consumers and in mental health services, clinicians often raise other concerns: that discussing religion with consumers feels intrusive, that it seems too personal, or that it metaphorically appears to violate the separation of church and state. The larger contemporary culture provides considerable support for such concerns. Religion is often pictured as a deeply personal matter—a thoroughly private domain of conscience (or realm between self and God)—about which open discussion is discouraged. In the context of professional relationships, however, an arena in which an individual's history of sexual or physical abuse, current intimate relationships and sexual activities, daily financial details, grooming, and illegal drug use are frequent topics of conversation, it is ironic indeed that spiritual experiences may be thought of as too personal.

Exploring clinicians' concerns in this regard has shown that the anxiety about religious talk often rests on personal rather than cultural grounds. For some professionals, their own painful histories with organized religion or its representatives make any religious discussion difficult. Some express a sense of inadequacy, a lack of training in the face of unfamiliar language, or a lack of knowledge sufficient to address spiritual concerns. Most psychologists in one survey, for example, indicated agreement with the statement, "Psychologists, in general, do not possess the knowledge or skills to assist individuals in their religious or spiritual development" (Shafranske and Malony, 1990, p. 75). Faced with occasional pressure to validate or invalidate religious experiences ("You do believe that was a miracle, don't you?"), many clinicians choose to avoid this kind of topic entirely.

This final concern, though, is an argument for additional professional education and supervision in addressing religion and spirituality, not for avoiding the topics altogether. Bolstering clinicians' understanding of, and skill in responding to, religious material is the most effective antidote to its neglect.

Reasons to Include Religion and Spirituality in Mental Health Services

Given the range of concerns just described, it is not surprising that little attention has been paid to the role of spirituality in services for people with severe mental illness. However, there are several persuasive reasons for considering that role.

Reflects Consumer Self-Understanding. Religion and spirituality are central to the self-understanding of many consumers. Even though data are relatively sparse on the fuller meanings of religious commitment among people with severe mental disorders, the data available indicate that this population does not differ markedly from the larger public. Kroll and Sheehan (1989) found broad consistency between the religious beliefs and practices of a group of psychiatric inpatients and the general public. In a Community Connections survey of one hundred consumers, 94 percent indicated a belief in God or a higher power. Only 1 percent considered themselves "not at all religious," whereas over 70 percent said they were "moderately," "considerably," or "very" religious. Further, over 80 percent agreed or strongly agreed with the statement, "It is important for me to spend time in prayer," and 70 percent reported praying at least weekly (Fallot and Azrin,1995). Because of the relatively greater involvement of African Americans in many aspects of religious activity (Gallup and Castelli, 1989), the large African American proportion of this sample may seem to inflate these figures. Other populations, however, indicate a similar commitment to religion or to spirituality. A survey of Eimer (1998) found parallel trends in a very different ethnic and regional group. Among predominantly white (65 percent) inpatients in a Michigan state psychiatric hospital, only 2 percent reported no belief in God, and 62 percent said they prayed at least weekly. Ritsher, Coursey, and Farrell (1997) note that many consumers spontaneously included religion among the most important "formative experiences" in their lives (following in frequency were relationships, work and accomplishments, and mental illness).

As is true for many other individuals, then, people with severe mental disorders may find in religion and spirituality deep sources of identity and meaning. Spirituality refers to who they *are* in addition to what they do and believe. For clinicians to minimize or avoid this dimension of experience, then, risks the neglect of a key aspect of self-definition for many consumers.

Facilitates Recovery. A second and closely related reason for including spirituality is that it may be central to the recovery experience of many consumers. Not only does religious commitment serve to clarify identity, it may function as a resource for personal and social strength (Fallot, 1997). As the paradigm of recovery (Anthony, 1993) has become more central in conceptualizing services for those with mental illness, emphases on enhanced self-esteem, greater empowerment, and a clearer sense of purpose have grown. Simultaneously, the necessity of looking at the full range of resources for recovery has also grown; spirituality is certainly prominent among these for many individuals. In Lindgren and Coursey's (1995) study, 80 percent of the consumer participants said that religion or spirituality had helped them in general, and 74 percent said that it helped when they were ill. Sullivan's interviews (1993) explore some of the reasons consumers give for their commitment to religion or spirituality, including strength for coping, social support, a sense of coherence, and the feeling of being a "whole person." Because recovery motifs are multidimensional and involve the entirety of an individual's life, it is not surprising that the encompassing realms of religion and spirituality may motivate, sustain, and consolidate the recovery process.

Enhances Cultural Sensitivity of Services. A third reason to include religion and spirituality in mental health services is the field's increasing awareness of the importance of culturally competent programming. In many cultural or subcultural and ethnic groups, religion and spirituality are especially vital sources of meaning and structure as well as healing. Many studies have pointed out, for example, the central role of black churches in the African American community (Lincoln and Mamiya, 1990). Pargament (1997a) has examined the greater use of religious coping mechanisms among those who are more religiously committed, including African Americans. He notes that religious coping, in turn, is most helpful for certain groups (blacks, the elderly, the poor, among others) who may have less access to other resources.

The clinician working with people from a cultural or ethnic group with strong religious beliefs and practices, then, needs to become knowledgeable about the function and meaning of these commitments. Mental health professions increasingly recognize this awareness as not only a clinical advantage but an ethical requirement. Most professional associations have established ethical codes that call for respect for the consumer's culture, and some specifically mention religion. Similarly, accreditation organizations increasingly recognize spiritual needs as part of an inclusive approach to services delivery.

Relates Positively to Psychosocial Well-Being. The final rationale for increased attention to religion and spirituality is an empirical one. On the whole, there exists a trend toward a slight but positive relationship between most measures of religion and most measures of mental health (Masters and Bergin, 1992). Gartner (1996) summarizes work that has generally found religion to be related to "hard" measures of mental health: religiousness is connected to lower rates of suicide, drug and alcohol use, and depression. The research in this field, then, calls for greater attention to the potentially positive role that religion may play in psychosocial well-being.

Conclusion

There are many reasons to expand the role of religion and spirituality in mental health services; among them are the following: these dimensions are central to the self-understanding and recovery experiences of many consumers; understanding religion's place in a particular culture is often essential to offering culturally competent services; and research indicates that religion is often related to more positive mental health outcomes. As comprehensive, empowerment-focused, and culturally attuned approaches to recovery and psychiatric rehabilitation become more widely adopted, the integration of spirituality can play a key role in mental health programs for people with severe mental disorders.

References

Anthony, W. A. "Recovery from Mental Illness: The Guiding Vision of the Mental Health Service System in the 1990s." *Psychosocial Rehabilitation Journal*, 1993, *16* (4), 11–23.

Browning, D. S. *Religious Thought and the Modern Psychologies: A Critical Conversation in the Theology of Culture.* Philadelphia: Fortress Press, 1987.

Diagnostic and Statistical Manual of Mental Disorders, Fourth Edition. Washington, D.C.: American Psychiatric Association, 1994.

Eimer, K. W. "Religiosity among Patients with Severe Mental Illness at a State Psychiatric Hospital." Unpublished manuscript, Ypsilanti Regional Psychiatric Hospital, Ypsilanti, Michigan, 1998.

Fallot, R. D. "Spirituality in Trauma Recovery." In M. Harris (ed.), *Sexual Abuse in the Lives of Women Diagnosed with Serious Mental Illness.* Amsterdam: Harwood Academic Publishers, 1997.

Fallot, R. D., and Azrin, S. T. "Consumer Satisfaction: Findings from a Case Management Program Evaluation Study." Paper presented at the Annual Conference of the International Association of Psychosocial Rehabilitation Services, Boston, June 1995.

Finke, R., and Stark, R. *The Churching of America: 1776–1990.* New Brunswick, N.J.: Rutgers University Press, 1992.

Fitchett, G., Burton, L. A., and Sivan, A. B. "The Religious Needs and Resources of Psychiatric Inpatients." *The Journal of Nervous and Mental Disease*, 1997, *185* (5), 320–326.

Freud, S. *Totem and Taboo.* New York: Norton, 1950. (Originally published 1913.)

Freud, S. *The Future of an Illusion.* Garden City, N.Y.: Anchor Books, 1964. (Originally published 1927.)

Gallup, G., Jr., and Castelli, J. *The People's Religion: American Faith in the 90s.* New York: Macmillan, 1989.

Gartner, J. "Religious Commitment, Mental Health, and Prosocial Behavior: A Review of the Empirical Literature." In E. F. Shafranske (ed.), *Religion and the Clinical Practice of Psychology.* Washington, D.C.: American Psychological Association, 1996.

Greer, B. A., and Roof, W. C. " 'Desperately Seeking Sheila': Locating Religious Privatism in American Society." *Journal for the Scientific Study of Religion*, 1992, *31* (3), 346–352.

Hastings, E. H., and Hastings, P. K. (eds.). *Index to International Public Opinion, 1994–95.* Westport, Conn.: Greenwood Press, 1996.

Koenig, H. G. *Aging and God: Spiritual Pathways to Mental Health in Midlife and Later Years.* New York: Haworth Press, 1994.

Koenig, H. G. *Handbook of Religion and Mental Health.* San Diego: Academic Press, 1998.

Kroll, J., and Sheehan, W. "Religious Beliefs and Practices Among 52 Psychiatric Inpatients in Minnesota." *American Journal of Psychiatry*, 1989, *146* (1), 67–72.

Lincoln, C. E., and Mamiya, L. H. *The Black Church in the African American Experience.* New York: Duke University Press, 1990.

Lindgren, K. N., and Coursey, R. D. "Spirituality and Serious Mental Illness: A Two-Part Study." *Psychosocial Rehabilitation Journal,* 1995, *18* (3), 93–111.

Lukoff, D., Lu, F., and Turner, R. "Toward a More Culturally Sensitive DSM-IV: Psychoreligious and Psychospiritual Problems." *The Journal of Nervous and Mental Disease,* 1992, *180* (11), 673–682.

Masters, K. S., and Bergin, A. E. "Religious Orientation and Mental Health." In J. F. Schumaker (ed.), *Religion and Mental Health.* New York: Oxford University Press, 1992.

Meissner, W. W. *Psychoanalysis and Religious Experience.* New Haven: Yale University Press, 1984.

Pargament, K. I. *The Psychology of Religion and Coping: Theory, Research, and Practice.* New York: Guilford Press, 1997a.

Pargament, K. I. "The Psychology of Religion *and* Spirituality? Yes and No." In M. J. Krejci (ed.), *Psychology of Religion Newsletter,* 1997b, *22* (3), 1–9.

Ragan, C., Malony, H. N., and Beit-Hallahmi, B. "Psychologists and Religion: Professional Factors and Personal Belief." *Review of Religious Research,* 1980, *21* (2), 208–217.

Ritsher, J.E.B., Coursey, R. D., and Farrell, E. W. "A Survey on Issues in the Lives of Women with Severe Mental Illness." *Psychiatric Services,* 1997, *48* (10), 1,273–1,282.

Schumaker, J. F. (ed.). *Religion and Mental Health.* New York: Oxford University Press, 1992.

Shafranske, E. F. (ed.). *Religion and the Clinical Practice of Psychology.* Washington, D.C.: American Psychological Association, 1996a.

Shafranske, E. F. "Religious Beliefs, Affiliations, and Practices of Clinical Psychologists." In E. F. Shafranske (ed.), *Religion and the Clinical Practice of Psychology.* Washington, D.C.: American Psychological Association, 1996b.

Shafranske, E. F., and Malony, H. N. "Clinical Psychologists' Religious and Spiritual Orientations and their Practice of Psychotherapy." *Psychotherapy,* 1990, *27* (1), 72–78.

Sperry, L., and Giblin, P. "Marital and Family Therapy with Religious Persons." In E. F. Shafranske (ed.), *Religion and the Clinical Practice of Psychology.* Washington, D.C.: American Psychological Association, 1996.

Sullivan, W. P. " 'It Helps Me to Be a Whole Person': The Role of Spirituality Among the Mentally Challenged." *Psychosocial Rehabilitation Journal,* 1993, *16* (3), 125–134.

Vande Kemp, H. "Historical Perspective: Religion and Clinical Psychology in America." In E. F. Shafranske (ed.), *Religion and the Clinical Practice of Psychology.* Washington, D.C.: American Psychological Association, 1996.

Wulff, D. W. "The Psychology of Religion: An Overview." In E. F. Shafranske (ed.), *Religion and the Clinical Practice of Psychology.* Washington, D.C.: American Psychological Association, 1996.

Zinnbauer, B. J., Pargament, K. I., Cole, B., Rye, M. S., Butter, E. M., Belavich, T. G., Hipp, K. M., Scott, A. B., and Kadar, J. L. "Religion and Spirituality: Unfuzzying the Fuzzy." *Journal for the Scientific Study of Religion,* 1997, *36* (4), 549–564.

ROGER D. FALLOT is co-director of Community Connections in Washington, D.C., and a member of the adjunct faculty in pastoral counseling at Loyola College in Maryland.

8

There is a core of services whose specific content varies from place to place that still appears to belong to the state mental hospital.

The State of the State Mental Hospital at the Turn of the Century

Leona L. Bachrach

In 1978, Maxwell Jones wrote, "I'm very worried about state hospitals, which I visit in many parts of the country. They are all demoralized and feel forgotten. The interest (and money) has moved to the new community programs which are not supplying the answer to chronic mental patients" (p. 610).

Over the past quarter-century, I have written at considerable length about the state of the state mental hospital in the United States. In a 1976 monograph entitled *Deinstitutionalization: An Analytical Review and Sociological Perspective* (Bachrach, 1976), I described the variety of functions, many of them subtle and unanticipated, that state mental hospitals had in the past performed and were continuing to execute even as community-based services were being rapidly developed. Some of those functions pertained to direct patient care; others had more to do with patients' families, service systems' priorities, and the demands of society at large. I suggested in that year that those functions were critical and could not productively be set aside, and I argued that successful deinstitutionalization would be dependent on communities' ability and willingness to assume the complete array of state mental hospital functions.

Ten years later in 1986, in an article in *Hospital and Community Psychiatry,* I wrote that although some communities had been more successful than others, the necessary transfer of state mental hospital functions to community agencies had been, at best, only partial (Bachrach, 1986b). I made four predictions—that the state hospital was destined to survive as an important service site for long-term mental patients into the foreseeable future; that, far from being monolithic, its character would vary greatly among states and communities; that it would continue to serve as one of a variety of important loci of care for long-term mental patients; and that it was destined to be burdened by identity crises and financial shortfalls in the years to come. I also urged that so long as the state mental hospital was serving as a vital force in service delivery, it should be viewed as an integral part of the continuum of services for those patients.

Today, as a new millennium dawns, I continue to hold these views—views that are bolstered by documentation in a corpus of literature that continues to grow in spite of what some experts perceive as a diminishing role for the state mental hospital: nothing I have witnessed or read over the past quarter-century leads me to alter these positions in any material way. Yet as I prepare this chapter, I find myself more reluctant than I formerly was to suggest what the future might hold for state mental hospitals. The profound changes in service delivery that have accompanied the growth of managed care in recent years have been occurring so rapidly that it is too early to say how mentally ill persons will ultimately fare (Bachrach, 1986b). That we are in the midst of a health care revolution in the United States is obvious, and I, for one, am loath to attempt to anticipate its consequences for individuals who suffer from severe and persisting mental illnesses.

The purposes of this chapter are twofold—to update my previous writings on the topic of state mental hospitals and to provide some perspective that may be of assistance to the next generation of service planners, who surely have their work cut out for them. Citations from the current literature—including periodical articles suggested in Medline searches, newspaper reports, recent books on mental health service systems, and a variety of writings found in the "fugitive" literature, which is generally unindexed in traditional archives—will be interspersed with commentary and observations born of long professional interest in, and personal concern for, the fate of persons who suffer from long-term mental illnesses.

Four general and interrelated questions that recur in today's literature serve as the basis for this analytical review. These revolve around prevailing contemporary perceptions of state mental hospitals, the characteristics of the patients whom those facilities serve, the fate of those whom they no longer serve, and the appropriate role of state hospitals in today's systems of care. Although these questions represent but a portion of those discussed in the literature, I have selected them for their currency and for the frequency with which they are voiced, either explicitly or implicitly. Their popularity reveals that the controversy over state hospital care has not died and that despite continued downsizing and depopulation of these facilities over more than forty years, experts are still pondering their value for patients, their relevance to the greater system of care, and their overall viability.

Four Interrelated Questions

In this section, each of the four questions is examined.

Question One. What is the prevailing view of state mental hospitals today, and how does it compare with the view that existed in the first half of this century?

This critical question may be paraphrased in more direct, perhaps less polite, terms: Are today's state mental hospitals "any better" than those that existed in the first half of this century? Are they more or less humane, and are the services they offer more or less appropriate? These are difficult questions to answer, for state mental hospitals in the past were very diverse facilities that varied greatly in their milieus, their treatment offerings, and the competence of their personnel; and they continue to be so to this day. Were the semanticist S. I. Hayakawa (1972) to have written about these facilities, he might well have said then, as now, that "state hospital is not state hospital." Some state mental hospitals today, as in the past, house innovative programs for the care and rehabilitation of long-term mental patients (Ozarin, 1989; Smith, 1998). Others serve as gateway facilities in integrated systems of care (Shapiro, 1983). Others, however, though generally attending to patients' basic survival needs, appear to offer them little that fosters effective treatment, personal hope, or growth.

What is more, there are no standardized, universally accepted criteria by which to assess the character or quality of a given state mental hospital, let alone to compare entire categories of these facilities over different time periods.

It is, however, possible to say that state mental hospitals in various parts of the United States are today under severe attack for reported nontherapeutic and inhumane practices, even as they were in the 1950s. For example, according to the *New York Times* ("New Managers . . . ," 1996, p. B5), a New Jersey state hospital recently experienced a "series of humiliating incidents," including patient suicides, staff negligence, and sexual assault of patients by staff members. In New York City in 1995, a violent, homicidal patient released from a state hospital pushed a woman to her death under a subway train—an incident that was widely viewed as the product of incompetent decision making within the hospital and that resulted in the dismissal of the state's acting commissioner of mental health (Dugger, 1995).

In the District of Columbia, patients at St. Elizabeths Hospital were forced for a period during the winter of 1995 to sleep in their coats because of a boiler malfunction (Harris, 1995). More recently, after a patient tumbled down a laundry chute to her death, St. Elizabeths was severely criticized for paying inadequate attention to the simple safety needs of its residents (Goldstein, 1997). A *Washington Post* article described that hospital as a place with "freezing wards, sporadic hot water, medication shortages, and inadequate staffing" (Strauss, 1996, p. A1, p. A5).

Similarly, the *Denver Post* asserted that the state mental hospital in Pueblo, in failing to provide individualized care for patients, had "triggered increases in the numbers of suicides, attempted suicides, assaults, sexual assaults and disciplinary measures involving seclusion or restraint" (Emery, Mitchell, and Lowe, 1998).

For many who recall the rhetoric of the early years of deinstitutionalization, there is a déjà vu quality both to these events and to the newspaper reports describing them: exposès of treatment deficits and inhumane living conditions inside state mental hospitals were common fare in those days. However, state mental hospitals even then had their supporters as well as their critics, and polarized views concerning the merits of deinstitutionalization were not uncommon.

By the early 1970s, it appeared that these views might be moderating (Bachrach, 1976). Dingman (1974) observed that many community-based facilities were being no more successful in meeting the needs of severely mentally ill individuals than were state hospitals, and he wrote that whatever the inherent problems of state hospital care might be, it was unthinkable to do away with them completely.

During the decade of the 1970s, concrete efforts to link state mental hospitals with community-based services in fact achieved some popularity in the United States in initiatives described as *unified systems of care* (Smith, Jones, and Coye, 1977; Stratas, Bernhardt, and Elwell, 1977; Talbott, 1983b). Perhaps, in retrospect, it was relatively easy in that decade to attempt to build systems of care that permitted the coexistence—even the active cooperation—of state mental hospitals and community-based agencies: it was a time when there seemed to be no limit to resources available for mental health services, and experimental initiatives were encouraged (Dinitz and Beran, 1971). But today's fierce competition for funding among mental health service entities (Freudenheim, 1995; Petrila, 1995) has led to something of a standoff, and it appears from the tenor of the most current literature that we are headed for a return to the either-or thinking of the early years of deinstitutionalization (Geller, 1997). I believe that part of the responsibility for this unfortunate situation lies in the indiscriminate condemnation of state hospital care by many decision makers—an ideological holdover from an earlier era (Jones, 1978).

There is, then, no single predominant view of state mental hospitals today. Polarized reactions to the services rendered in these facilities—and even to their very presence as operating service sites for the care of long-term mental patients—prevail; and any progress, real or apparent, that might once have been made in bringing opposing views closer together is, at best, in abeyance.

Nor can we make valid comparisons between the state mental hospitals of today and yesteryear. Because we lack standardized criteria that would enable us to undertake such comparisons in any global manner, we are destined to abide by the limits imposed by historical canon; and we must assess these facilities only within, not across, time periods.

Question Two. What individuals tend to be served in state mental hospitals today?

Numerically speaking, the position of the state mental hospital in the spectrum of services for long-term mental patients has declined significantly over the past four decades (National Association of State Mental Health Program Directors, 1997; Witkin, Atay, and Manderscheid, 1996). Over a period of about forty years, there was a drop of approximately 86 percent in the number of resident patients in those facilities—from 560,000 people in 1955 to 77,000 people in the early years of this decade. Even more impressive is the decrease in resident patient rates: in 1955, 339 out of every 100,000 people living in the United States resided in state mental hospitals; early in this decade, only 31 of every 100,000 people were on those hospitals' rolls on any given day—a drop of well over 90 percent (Bachrach, 1986a; Center for Mental Health Services, 1995a).

Additional documentation for the declining presence of the state mental hospital in numerical terms is provided by comparative statistics on the location of patient care episodes. In 1955, 63 percent of all such episodes in the United States were conducted in state mental hospitals, in contrast to only 16 percent in 1990 (Redick, Witkin, Atay, and Manderscheid, 1994).

To some critics of the passing scene, the fact that more than 75,000 individuals continue to reside in state mental hospitals on any given day is probably regarded as excessive and as evidence that deinstitutionalization—the replacement of state mental hospitals with an array of community-based facilities for the care of severely mentally ill individuals (Bachrach, 1976)—has progressed neither far enough nor rapidly enough. To others, however, this figure establishes something of a threshold for the absolute limits of deinstitutionalization: it suggests that there is an irreducible minimum beyond which state mental hospital populations will not drop (Lamb, 1997; Thompson and others, 1993; Wines, 1988). To still others who view with alarm the growing populations of poorly served or totally unserved mentally ill individuals in our correctional facilities and on our streets (Butterfield, 1998; Center for Mental Health Services, 1995b; Friedrich and Flory, 1996; Isaac and Jaffe, 1996; Lamb and Weinberger, 1998; Lurigio and Lewis, 1989; Munetz and Geller, 1993; Satel, 1996; Teplin, 1990; Torrey, 1995), the number is perhaps far too small and might productively be increased to accommodate the needs of individuals who are largely overlooked in today's community-based systems of care.

Who is represented among the individuals who continue to use our state mental hospitals today? The actual number of users over the course of a year is substantially larger than the resident count on any one day; and generally speaking, the rolls of those facilities include, as they did in the past, measurable numbers of people in three major subgroups (Bachrach, 1978; Craig, Goodman, Siegel, and Wanderling, 1984; Wing, 1975):

Old long-stay patients—individuals who have resided in the hospital for an extended period of time, generally more than one year but often in excess

of five or ten years, and who are considered to be "poor risks" for discharge
New long-stay patients—recent first admissions who are unlikely to be
released to the community
Short-stay patients—recently admitted patients who are likely to remain in
residence for periods of only one or two weeks or even less and who often
return to be readmitted in a "revolving-door" manner

Short-stay patients, particularly those with multiple admissions, represent
a clear majority in many if not most facilities (Appleby and others, 1993;
Fisher and others, 1996; Geller, 1992). However, the precise composition
of state hospital populations varies greatly from facility to facility, and there
are probably as many answers to the question of who is on the rolls of the
state mental hospital as there are state hospitals. The sources of variance are
complex, but several intertwined prominent conditions stand out.

First, the characteristics of mentally ill persons living in the geographic
area served by a particular hospital must be taken into account. What is the
distribution of these individuals according to diagnosis, symptomatology,
level of functioning, demographic characteristics, ability to tolerate stress,
and individual treatment history? Is the locale attracting transient severely
mentally ill persons? Does it contain many homeless mentally ill people?
Because all of these circumstances play a critical role in service utilization
patterns, their distribution within the base population will to some extent
determine who is admitted to, and who stays inside, a given state mental
hospital.

Second, laws and regulations governing both inpatient and outpatient
civil commitment of mentally ill persons vary among states, and these too
have an influence on the composition of a state mental hospital's resident
population (Isaac and Jaffe, 1996; Geller, 1986). In some catchment areas,
the legal criteria for hospital admission, often restricted to dangerousness
to one's self or others, are extremely rigid; and the "front doors" to those
facilities are practically impossible to penetrate—a situation that has caused
some service providers as well as family advocacy groups to react with dis-
may (Carr, 1992; Foderaro, 1994; Jaffe, 1995). Some state mental hospitals
limit their admissions to involuntary commitments, but others—those
located in communities that are relatively relaxed about admission criteria—
contain greater percentages of people who have been voluntarily admitted.
Some hospitals are actually reported to open their doors, albeit temporarily,
to transient mentally ill persons who have traveled considerable distances
from their homes (Bachrach, 1988b).

A third set of variables affecting who uses the state hospital today is
related to the array of alternative services actually available to severely mentally ill persons within the community. Individual places differ greatly in
their service offerings as well as their gatekeeping practices; and to the
extent that community agencies function as "trade-offs" for state hospitals,

they too will influence the nature of the hospital's population. Some experts are persuaded that the emergence of managed care entities is today gravely limiting long-term patients' access to traditional services, both within the community and in state hospitals (Pinheiro, 1998).

Finally, a fourth set of circumstances that is critical in determining state hospital utilization patterns has to do with the community's goals in serving mentally ill individuals. Some communities are apparently less willing than others to tolerate the presence of these individuals (Lamb, Bachrach, and Kass, 1992). Some, for example, may be particularly sensitive to the existence of unserved, often homeless, mentally ill persons in their midst, and those that wish to minimize the presence of this population often turn to the state mental hospital as an alternative to providing no care at all. In some cases, the community's motives for using the state hospital in this manner may simply be intolerance and discrimination; in other instances, however, the hospital may genuinely be seen as a humane option for relieving the discomfort and pain experienced by many severely mentally ill persons in the community.

In a similar vein, the state mental hospital in some places has become the predominant treatment site for individuals who are violent, who appear to be dangerous to themselves or others, who have a history of incarceration, who are perceived as unable to care for themselves, or who are in some sense regarded as public nuisances. Numerous reports in the literature provide important clues to the characteristics of such "difficult-to-serve" individuals, who, not infrequently, end up on the state hospital's rolls in the absence of other facilities that will treat them (Bigelow and others, 1988; Casper, 1995; Fisher and others, 1996; Geller, 1992; Holohean, Banks, and Maddy, 1993; Lyons and others, 1997; Sederer and Summergrad, 1993).

Question Three. What has been the fate of those mentally ill persons who are no longer served in state mental hospitals?

In the past, "chronic mental patient" was considered to be acceptable terminology and was commonly used to refer to people who were enrolled in state mental hospitals (Bachrach, 1988a). In my 1976 monograph, I defined chronic mental patients as "those persons who are, have been, or might have been, but for the deinstitutionalization movement, on the rolls of state mental hospitals" (1976, p. 1). Today, sensitized to the distress that this term causes to many people who suffer from severe and persisting mental illnesses (Bachrach, 1992a, 1993b), I often attempt to substitute other language for this term. Yet the definition I offered in 1976 precisely captures the focus of this third question.

Once again, there are no simple answers. Many of these persons have, according to a variety of outcome indices, been successfully treated in community-based service settings (Cohen, 1990; Dincin, 1995; Warner, 1995), although, as in the case of resident state hospital populations, percentages differ greatly among communities in accord with the variables discussed earlier in this chapter. For these persons, the basic philosophy of deinstitutionalization—the notion that community care is more humane and more therapeutic than state mental hospital care (Bachrach, 1976)—is demonstrably valid, for the quality of their treatment and of their lives is vastly improved over that in state mental hospitals. Many of these individuals express much greater satisfaction with their life circumstances when those are contrasted with conditions inside the hospitals, and indeed some patients, in spite of their illnesses, have realized a certain degree of "normalization" in their daily activities. Some live independently and some are productively employed, achievements that were relatively rare in the days when state mental hospitals dominated our systems of care.

But these generalizations apply only to some mentally ill individuals. Other persons who might in the past have resided in state mental hospitals have been discharged to communities where there are few if any programs to serve them (Wong, 1997), and many end up living on the streets. Others—an ever growing percentage of the total population of persons suffering from long-term mental illnesses—have never been admitted to state mental hospitals, nor any other treatment facilities, in the first place (Bachrach, 1978, 1992b), often as the result of so-called "admission diversion" policies (Geller, 1992), which are sometimes little more than a euphemism for providing no care at all (Dionne, 1978; Sullivan, 1979).

Even in those places where community care has been thoughtfully conceived and adequately funded—even in service systems where great hope, effort, and clinical competence have been invested in community-based enterprises—some mentally ill persons are inadequately treated or entirely untreated (Dewees, Pulice, and McCormick, 1996). For example, some so-called "*new* chronic patients" have found it extremely difficult to sustain themselves in the community. Among other problems, their easy access to alcohol and other chemical substances has greatly exacerbated their psychiatric symptoms and interfered with any progress they might otherwise have made in community-based care (Bachrach, 1996a; Lamb and Shaner, 1993; Satel, 1996).

Somewhere between one-third and one-half of the nation's homeless individuals reportedly suffer from long-term mental illnesses (Lamb, Bachrach, and Kass, 1992). One recent estimate from Denver, Colorado, places the percentage at between 50 and 60 percent (Callahan, 1998). Many of these individuals would surely, in the past, have been served in state mental hospitals. Whether they are "better off" on the streets is a matter of personal judgment, although it is fair to say that at a minimum, their basic needs for food, shelter, clothing, and medical care would be met more readily within the hospital setting (Belkin, 1992).

Another significant portion of the population previously served in state mental hospitals can, as previously noted, be found in jails and other correctional facilities. Many of these individuals experience great difficulties in linking up with the mental health service system after their release.

How can we explain these disturbing circumstances in view of the early promise that community care held for mentally ill individuals? The plight of these underserved and unserved persons must in some part be attributed to such factors as community resistance to their integration into society, severe fragmentation in community-based service systems, and persistent funding problems (Bachrach, 1997; Bachrach and Lamb, 1989). Further complications doubtless arise from the fact that nothing in the world of mental health service planning stands still for long, a fact that makes it difficult to plan, justify, and sustain new programs. Old service structures disappear, and new service delivery practices are introduced, even as political support for improving mental health care in the nation grows increasingly uncertain (Bachrach 1991, 1997). Even the language of mental health service delivery changes dramatically in response to promises implied in "quick-fix" treatment concepts (Bachrach, 1994).

Thus, it is hardly surprising that state and local governments faced with the need to respond to a multitude of special-interest groups have largely lacked the resources—and often, as well, the interest and will—to attend adequately to the needs of long-term mental patients (Kammer, 1995; Sowers, 1995; Wolpert, 1995). The irony in this situation is that now that we have considerable experience to guide us in future efforts to supplant state mental hospitals with alternative community-based facilities, we are faced with the reality that the care of mentally ill people is not merely a matter of social conscience and professional skill. It is also, unfortunately, very much a matter of politics and of changing service priorities. The idealism and hope of the 1960s—when community care was widely endorsed and aggressively pursued (and when funding seemed ever to be available)—has, at least temporarily, given way to more mundane considerations of cost containment in the design of mental health service systems (Bachrach, 1996b; Petrila, 1995; Pinheiro, 1998).

How then can we sum up the response to this third question? I would submit, first, that the fate of people no longer served in state mental hospitals has been so varied that it is difficult to make any summary judgment about their circumstances, or even about their whereabouts. Some have fared admirably; others have experienced living conditions at least as undesirable, and sometimes more life threatening and inhumane, as what they might have known as state hospital residents. And although we now have considerable technology for improving the care of these underserved individuals—in the form of case-finding techniques, outreach and case management services, an array of residential opportunities, rehabilitation interventions, and specialized dual diagnosis programs (Carling, 1993; Cohen, 1990; Dincin, 1995; Warner, 1995; Zealberg, Santos, and Fisher, 1993)—their fate, given today's political climate and shrinking resources, is at best an embarrassment to the mental health community and society at large and at worst an unqualified tragedy for them and their families.

Is it then time to reinstate our state mental hospitals as the central loci in our system of care? There is no clear-cut answer to this question, for it is largely a matter of judgment: one's own personal convictions must be considered. It is, however, important to note that on the one hand, the motives of those who call for a renaissance of state hospital care are often humane and should not be dismissed as necessarily reactionary (Dumont, 1995; Isaac and Jaffe, 1995; Lamb, 1992; Lamb and Shaner, 1993; Zaleski, Gale, and Winget, 1979). On the other hand, those who are disposed to view the cup of deinstitutionalization as being half full rather than half empty are for their part justified in fearing that a massive return to state hospital care at this juncture would undermine the slow but very real progress that we have made in building community-based mental health systems (Bachrach, 1997).

Both excellent and inferior treatment and care are found in both kinds of service settings, and neither can be described unqualifiedly as inherently better for all patients under all circumstances. Thus, efforts to reach productive coexistence are definitely in order at this time. It is important that we attempt once again, as we did during the early 1970s, to depolarize extreme views on the issue of state mental hospital care. People whose lives have been thwarted by severe mental illness must not be further victimized by the intransigence of ideologues or by the political correctness (Lamb, 1994; Wilson, 1993) of pragmatists.

Question Four. What is an appropriate role for the state mental hospital in today's uncertain and rapidly changing systems of care?

It is not sufficient to acknowledge that state mental hospitals continue to occupy a critical niche within the systems of care in many communities; we must go further and attempt to describe that niche even though this task is fraught with risks. Trying to outline the state mental hospital's proper place within the mental health system too often encourages us to play "geography games," in which the hospital is viewed as a collection of bricks and mortar and not as a facility—in some places the only facility—that provides specific services for mentally ill individuals.

The rules of geography games are not subtle; the winner is the person who supports any facility other than the state mental hospital, which, ideologically, is still widely viewed as inherently undesirable. Planners are, in fact, encouraged to play geography games whenever their programs are evaluated according to commonly used indices of hospital tenure—such as declines in numbers of admissions, resident patients, and length of stay—as outcome criteria. More subtle measures of appropriateness of services, quality of care, and quality of life (Bachrach, 1997; Kincheloe, 1997; Munetz and Geller, 1993) give the players in these games relatively few points.

Geography games are popular, partly because they simplify very complex events, and several steps must be taken to guard against their seductiveness. First, planners and service providers must acknowledge that despite the existence of model systems of community care in some selected American communities, the growth of community-based services in this country has thus far failed to eliminate the need for state mental hospitals (Kincheloe, 1997; van Norman and Stone, 1996). The issue, if one reads carefully between the lines in contributions to the literature, is not so much whether the community has the potential for providing a full array of services (Becker and Schulberg, 1976; Dincin and others, 1993; Okin, 1995) but rather whether it possesses the resources and the will to do so. Absent these critical ingredients, state hospital care must still be viewed as an essential element in any array of comprehensive services.

By focusing on service statistics as major outcome indices, geography games tend to discourage us from looking as closely as we might at what it is that state mental hospitals actually do. Thus, a second important step in guarding against those games is to assess the full array of services that these facilities provide (Bopp and Fisher, 1995; Munetz and Geller, 1993; Townsend and Seiden, 1987). The literature reveals that state mental hospitals actually fulfill an amazing array of functions. Not only do they typically monitor the course of illness among severely disabled individuals, but they also provide psychiatric treatment, medical care, rehabilitation, short- and long-term asylum, residential care, crisis intervention, social structure, and role definition (Bachrach, 1976, 1984; Kincheloe, 1997; Smith, 1998; Wasow, 1993). This is not to say that all hospitals necessarily render all of these services nor even that they always offer the most desirable options. However, in many places state mental hospitals may well be the only facilities that provide even the most minimal care and asylum to persons in grave need of assistance. In those instances, it is the patients who are the real losers in geography games.

Furthermore, it is not solely patients who are served by state mental hospitals. For their relatives, the hospital may provide much needed respite and relief, as well as education and support (Craig and others, 1987). For the system of care, it may provide a venue where those individuals who appear to be most difficult to reach can be engaged in treatment. For the professional community, the hospital may afford unparalleled opportunities for research and training (Douglas and others, 1994; Miller, 1981). For society, it may serve as a place for segregating and confining dangerous individuals. And for local communities, particularly those located in rural areas, the state mental hospital may provide a tax base and a critical locus of employment.

This partial listing of state hospital functions (Bachrach, 1976) provides some clues to the proper role of those facilities in today's system of care in any particular community. Were the hospital merely a place for psychiatric and medical treatment, its functions could easily be supplanted by other short- or long-term treatment facilities in the community. Were it only a place of detention, its functions could readily be taken over by the criminal justice system. Were it merely a residential site for severely ill individuals, it could easily be replaced by an array of graded housing facilities. And although community-based agencies in some places have performed one or more, perhaps even all, of these functions with notable success, no single class of service entities has yet been able to match the state hospital for multifunctionality.

In summary, however well or poorly any individual hospital may execute the functions with which it has become identified—however inhumane the living conditions within it or however enlightened the treatment—there is a core of services whose specific content varies from place to place that still appears to belong to the state mental hospital. Recognizing this fact is not necessarily tantamount to endorsing the hospital's indefinite existence; it is merely a statement of reality. The British psychiatrist John Wing (1975) has eloquently summed up the concept by which the state mental hospital's role must be assessed:

> The quality of life lived by the patient and his relatives is the final criterion by which services must be judged. A good hospital is better than a poor hostel or a poor family environment. A good family environment is better than a poor hospital or a poor hostel. The same may be said of day-time environments— open employment, enclaves in ordinary commercial business, rehabilitation or sheltered workshops, or protected day centers. Universal denunciation of any one type of setting is likely to be harmful since it is clearly not based on rational principles of assessment, treatment or care [p. 254].

It is perhaps also relevant to mention—although I do so reluctantly, for I have never felt that cost should be the bottom line in planning services for those in need—that the downsizing of state mental hospitals has not uniformly resulted in cost savings (Hollingsworth and Sweeney, 1997; Okin, 1995), as so many early proponents of deinstitutionalization had anticipated, and as some service planners continue to assume today ("Help for the Mentally Ill," 1993; Swidler and Tauriello, 1995). In many instances, *cost shifting* may be a more accurate description of reality than cost savings (Kane, 1995), for the comprehensive care of severely disabled persons tends to be expensive no matter where it takes place; and as Thornicroft and Bebbington (1989) have noted, the more comprehensive and methodologically sophisticated a cost analysis is, the less certain it appears that community-based services are cheaper than those provided in mental hospitals.

Unified Systems of Care

All things considered, perhaps the time has come to reintroduce the notion of unified systems of care into our service-planning efforts, particularly in this era of managed care when the execution of many state hospital functions has been severely threatened (Lazarus, 1994; Minkin, Stoline, and Sharfstein, 1994). Popular in the 1950s and 1960s, these initiatives, described by John Talbott (1983b) as "utopian," were ahead of their time: they proved to be too threatening to vested political interests, and they severely challenged established notions of appropriateness in resource allocation.

Are we more nearly ready to acknowledge their merits today? At least in theory, a unified system of care makes a proper assessment of the needs of all service users, enrolled or potential, in the catchment area (Glick, Klar, and Braff, 1984). Medical and psychiatric "necessity" is defined in the broadest possible way to include treatment, rehabilitation, and support service needs; and to the extent that it is feasible to do so, the collateral needs of persons other than patients—for example, family members—are also considered. However, the patient's welfare remains the central focus in the planning process.

Once levels of need have been assessed, the planning task becomes a matter of evaluating the availability of services for meeting those needs. Ideally, the state mental hospital should, like any other agency in the system of care, provide those services that it performs best, whether they fall into the realm of medical and psychiatric treatment, vocational training, day treatment, asylum care, or any other class of interventions. Duplication of services among agencies should be avoided whenever possible.

In this paradigm, it is essential that the state mental hospital not be considered a facility of last resort (Geller, 1991; Rachlin, Grossman, and Frankel, 1979; Spiro, 1982)—one where patients whom no other facility wants are "dumped"—but rather a full partner among agencies in the system of care (Rothbard and others, 1998). Appelbaum (1991) has aptly noted that in many instances, inferior care in state hospitals has become a self-fulfilling prophesy, because those facilities are unable to establish control over admission decisions and must accept as their lot whoever and whatever is handed to them. Including hospital representatives in systemwide planning meetings and communitywide case conferences, helpful mechanisms for ensuring interagency partnership and cooperation (Bachrach, 1993a), is too often overlooked and should be aggressively encouraged. Case management activities should not be confined to concerns affecting a single agency but should be systemwide, so that the case manager–patient relationship can flourish whether the individual is living in the hospital or in the community.

Utopian? Perhaps. Idealistic? Definitely. Essential? Decidedly. Practicable? Yes—but only with great effort and cooperation from the political powers that be. Talbott (1983a) clearly outlined the rationale for unified systems of care in 1983, and his reasoning makes a great deal of sense today, particularly with the growth of managed care ("Help for the Mentally Ill," 1993). Like Talbott, I hold hope for the future and believe, like him, that "states and regions, haltingly but steadily, will continue to move away from the current fragmentation of mental health services and toward coordination and integration, if not unification, of all services" (p. 111). This much we owe to those individuals who rely on our service systems for treatment, rehabilitation, support, and often basic survival.

References

Appelbaum, P. "Barring the State Hospital Door." *Hospital and Community Psychiatry*, 1991, *42*(4), 351–352.

Appleby, L., and others. "Length of Stay and Recidivism in Schizophrenia: A Study of Public Psychiatric Hospital Patients." *American Journal of Psychiatry*, 1993, *150*(1), 72–76.

Bachrach, L. *Deinstitutionalization: An Analytical Review and Sociological Perspective.* Rockville, Md.: National Institute of Mental Health, 1976.

Bachrach, L. "A Conceptual Approach to Deinstitutionalization." *Hospital and Community Psychiatry,* 1978, 29(9), 573–578.

Bachrach, L. "Asylum and Chronically Ill Psychiatric Patients." *American Journal of Psychiatry,* 1984, 141(8), 975–978.

Bachrach, L. "Deinstitutionalization: What Do the Numbers Mean?" *Hospital and Community Psychiatry,* 1986a, 37(2), 118–119, 121.

Bachrach, L. "The Future of the State Mental Hospital." *Hospital and Community Psychiatry,* 1986b, 37(5), 467–474.

Bachrach, L. "Defining Chronic Mental Illness: A Concept Paper." *Hospital and Community Psychiatry,* 1988a, 39(4), 383–388.

Bachrach, L. "Transient Patients in a Western State Hospital." *Hospital and Community Psychiatry,* 1988b, 39(2), 123–124.

Bachrach, L. "The 13th Principle." *Hospital and Community Psychiatry,* 1991, 42(12), 1205–1206.

Bachrach, L. "'The Chronic Patient': In Search of a Title." *Hospital and Community Psychiatry,* 1992a, 43(9), 867–868.

Bachrach, L. "What We Know About Homelessness Among Mentally Ill Persons: An Analytical Review and Commentary." *Hospital and Community Psychiatry,* 1992b, 43(5), 453–464.

Bachrach, L. "Organizational Issues and Expertise in Care Innovation: Applying the Principles of Continuity of Care." In J. Wolf and J. van Weeghel (eds.), *Changing Community Psychiatry: Care Innovation for Persons with Long-Term Mental Illness in The Netherlands.* Utrecht: Netherlands Institute of Mental Health, 1993a.

Bachrach, L. "Should 'The Chronic Patient' Be Replaced? Reader Responses." *Hospital and Community Psychiatry,* 1993b, 44(9), 817–818.

Bachrach, L. "The Semantics of Mental Health Service Delivery." Paper presented at the 47th annual meeting of the Ontario Psychiatric Association, Toronto, Jan. 28, 1994.

Bachrach, L. "Deinstitutionalization: Promises, Problems, and Prospects." In H. Knudsen and G. Thornicroft (eds.), Mental *Health Service Evaluation.* Cambridge, England: Cambridge University Press, 1996a.

Bachrach, L . "Managed Care: Some 'Latent Functions.'" *Psychiatric Services,* 1996b, 47(3), 243–244.

Bachrach, L. "Lessons from the American Experience in Providing Community-Based Services." In J. Leff (ed.), *Caring in the Community: Illusion or Reality?* Chichester, England: Wiley, 1997.

Bachrach, L., and Lamb, H. "What Have We Learned from Deinstitutionalization?" *Psychiatric Annals,* 1989, 19(1), 12–21.

Becker, A., and Schulberg, H. "Phasing Out State Hospitals: A Psychiatric Dilemma." *New England Journal of Medicine,* 1976, 294(5), 255–261.

Belkin, L. "Treating the Sick Can Mean Clothing Them Too." *New York Times,* Nov. 24, 1992, pp. B1–B2.

Bigelow, D., and others. "Characteristics of State Hospital Patients Who Are Hard to Place." *Hospital and Community Psychiatry,* 1988, 39(2), 181–185.

Bopp, J., and Fisher, W. "The State Psychiatric Center as an Academically Affiliated Tertiary Care Hospital." *Psychiatric Quarterly,* 1995, 66(3), 237–247.

Butterfield, F. "Prisons Replace Hospitals for the Nation's Mentally Ill." *New York Times,* Mar. 5, 1998, p. A1, p. A26.

Callahan, P. "Colorado Mentally Ill Count a Mystery." *Denver Post Online,* [http://www.denverpost.com]. Aug. 16, 1998.

Carling, P. "Housing and Supports for Persons with Mental Illness: Emerging Approaches to Research and Practice." *Hospital and Community Psychiatry,* 1993, 44(4), 439–449.

Carr, A. "The Scary Situation in Our Shelters." *Washington Post*, Dec. 13, 1992, p. C8.

Casper, E. "Identifying Multiple Recidivists in a State Hospital Population." *Psychiatric Services*, 1995, 46(10), 1074–1075.

Center for Mental Health Services. *Additions and Resident Patients at End of Year, State and County Mental Hospitals, by Age and Diagnosis, by State, United States, 1993.* Rockville Md.: Substance Abuse and Mental Health Services Administration, 1995a.

Center for Mental Health Services. *Double Jeopardy: Persons with Mental Illnesses in the Criminal Justice System: A Report to Congress.* Rockville Md.: Substance Abuse and Mental Health Services Administration, 1995b.

Cohen, N. (ed.). *Psychiatry Takes to the Streets.* New York: Guilford Press, 1990.

Craig, T., Goodman, M., Siegel, C., and Wanderling, J. "The Dynamics of Hospitalization in a Defined Population During Deinstitutionalization." *American Journal of Psychiatry*, 1984, 141(6), 782–785.

Craig, T., and others. "Family Support Programs in a Regional Mental Health System." *Hospital and Community Psychiatry*, 1987, 38(5), 459–460.

Dewees, M., Pulice, R., and McCormick, L. "Community Integration of Former State Hospital Patients: Outcomes of a Policy Shift in Vermont." *Psychiatric Services*, 1996, 47(10), 1088–1092.

Dincin, J. (ed.). *A Pragmatic Approach to Psychiatric Rehabilitation: Lessons from Chicago's Thresholds Program.* New Directions for Mental Health Services, no. 68. San Francisco: Jossey-Bass, 1995.

Dincin, J., and others. "Impact of Assertive Community Treatment on the Use of State Hospital Inpatient Bed-Days." *Hospital and Community Psychiatry*, 1993, 44(9), 833–838.

Dingman, P. "The Case for the State Mental Hospital." *Where Is My Home: Proceedings of a Conference on the Closing of State Mental Hospitals, Scottsdale, Arizona, February 14–15, 1974.* Menlo Park, Calif.: Stanford Research Institute, 1974.

Dinitz, S, and Beran, N. "Community Mental Health as a Boundaryless and Boundary-Busting System." *Journal of Health and Social Behavior*, 1971, 12(1), 99–108.

Dionne, E. "Mental Patient Cutbacks Planned." *New York Times*, Dec. 8, 1978, p. B3.

Douglas, E., and others. "A Ten-Year Update of Administrative Relationships Between State Hospitals and Academic Psychiatry Departments." *Hospital and Community Psychiatry*, 1994, 45(11), 1113–1116.

Dugger, C. "State Called Patient Violent, Then Let Him Roam." *New York Times*, Jan. 7, 1995, p. 1, p. 26.

Dumont, M. "Our Lady of the State Hospital." *Readings: A Journal of Reviews and Commentary in Mental Health*, 1995, 10(4), 8–11.

Emery, E., Mitchell, K., and Lowe, P. "Records Show Mental Hospital Fails to Give Individualized Care." *Denver Post Online*, [http://www.denverpost.com]. Aug. 16, 1998.

Fisher, W., and others. "Case Mix in the 'Downsizing' State Hospitals." *Psychiatric Services*, 1996, 47(3), 255–262.

Foderaro, L. "Mental Hospitals for Unwilling Gain Support in New York State." *New York Times*, June 17, 1994, p. A1, p. B4.

Freudenheim, M. "States Shelving Ambitious Plans on Health Care." *New York Times*, Jul. 2, 1995, p. 1, p. 20.

Friedrich, R., and Flory, C. "Is There Hope for Those Who Require Long-Term Care?" *Newsletter of the National Alliance for the Mentally Ill Advocate*, Mar.–Apr. 1996, p. 4.

Geller, J. "Rights, Wrongs, and the Dilemma of Coerced Community Treatment." *American Journal of Psychiatry*, 1986, 143(10), 1259–1264.

Geller, J. "'Anyplace but the State Hospital': Examining Assumptions About the Benefits of Admission Diversion." *Hospital and Community Psychiatry*, 1991, 42(2), 145–152.

Geller, J. "A Report on the 'Worst' State Hospital Recidivists in the U.S." *Hospital and Community Psychiatry*, 1992, 43(9), 904–908.

Geller, J. "We Still Count Beds." *Psychiatric Services*, 1997, 48(10), 1233.

Glick, I., Klar, H., and Braff, D. "Guidelines for Hospitalization of Chronic Psychiatric Patients." *Hospital and Community Psychiatry*, 1984, 35(9), 934–936.

Goldstein, A. "St. Elizabeths Accreditation in Jeopardy." *Washington Post*, Apr. 2, 1997, p. B1, p. B7.

Harris, H. "Boiler Failure Limits Heat at St. Elizabeths." *Washington Post*, Dec. 12, 1995, p. E6.

Hayakawa, S. I. *Language in Thought and Action.* (3rd ed.) Orlando: Harcourt Brace, 1972.

"Help for the Mentally Ill." *New York Times,* July 3, 1993, p. 18.

Hollingsworth, E., and Sweeney, J. "Mental Health Expenditures for People with Severe Mental Illnesses." *Psychiatric Services*, 1997, 48(4), 485–490.

Holohean, E., Banks, S., and Maddy, B. "Patient Subgroups in State Psychiatric Hospitals and Implications for Administration." *Hospital and Community Psychiatry*, 1993, 44(10), 1002–1004.

Isaac, R. J., and Jaffe, D. J. "Mental Illness, Public Safety." *New York Times*, Dec. 23, 1995, p. 27.

Isaac, R., and Jaffe, D. "Committed to Help." *National Review*, Jan. 29, 1996, pp. 34–38.

Jaffe, D. "Change Involuntary Treatment Laws." *Newsletter of the National Alliance for the Mentally Ill Advocate,* Jan.–Feb. 1995, pp. 16–21.

Jones, M. "State Mental Hospitals: Demoralized, Forgotten?" *Hospital and Community Psychiatry*, 1978, 29(9), 610.

Kammer, F. "Block Grants Will Worsen Poverty." *New York Times*, Aug. 1, 1995, p. A15.

Kane, C. "Deinstitutionalization and Managed Care: Déjà Vu?" *Psychiatric Services*, 1995, 46(9), 883–889.

Kincheloe, M. "A State Mental Health System with No State Hospital: The Vermont Plan Ten Years Later." *Psychiatric Services,* 1997, 48(8), 1078–1080.

Lamb, H. "Is It Time for a Moratorium on Deinstitutionalization?" *Hospital and Community Psychiatry*, 1992, 43(7), 669.

Lamb, H. "Only Good News Is Politically Correct." *Hospital and Community Psychiatry*, 1994, 45(6), 17.

Lamb, H. "The New State Mental Hospitals in the Community." *Psychiatric Services,* 1997, 48(10), 1307.

Lamb, H., Bachrach, L., and Kass, F. (eds.). *Treating the Homeless Mentally Ill: A Report of the Task Force on the Homeless Mentally Ill.* Washington, D.C.: American Psychiatric Association, 1992.

Lamb, H., and Shaner, R. "When There Are Almost No State Hospital Beds Left." *Hospital and Community Psychiatry,* 1993, 44(10), 973–976.

Lamb, H., and Weinberger, L. "Persons with Severe Mental Illness in Jails and Prisons: A Review." *Psychiatric Services*, 1998, 49(4), 483–492.

Lazarus, A. "Managed Care: Lessons from Community Mental Health." *Psychiatric Services*, 1994, 45(4), 301.

Lurigio, A., and Lewis, D. "Worlds That Fail: A Longitudinal Study of Urban Mental Patients." *Journal of Social Issues,* 1989, 45(1), 79–90.

Lyons, J., and others. "Predicting Readmission to the Psychiatric Hospital in a Managed Care Environment: Implications for Quality Indicators." *American Journal of Psychiatry*, 1997, 154(3), 337–340.

Miller, R. "Beyond the Old State Hospital: New Opportunities Ahead." *Hospital and Community Psychiatry*, 1981, 32(1), 27–31.

Minkin, E., Stoline, A., and Sharfstein, S. "An Analysis of the Two-Class System of Care in Public and Private Psychiatric Hospitals." *Hospital and Community Psychiatry*, 1994, 45(10), 975–977.

Munetz, M., and Geller J. "The Least Restrictive Alternative in the Postinstitutional Era." *Hospital and Community Psychiatry*, 1993, 44(10), 967–973.

National Association of State Mental Health Program Directors. *Closing and Reorganizing State Psychiatric Hospitals: 1996.* State Mental Health Agency Profile System Highlights, no. 1. Alexandria, Va.: National Association of State Mental Health Program Directors, Dec. 1997.

"New Managers to Take Over Troubled Psychiatric Hospital." *New York Times*, Feb. 5, 1996, p. B5.

Okin, R. "Testing the Limits of Deinstitutionalization." *Psychiatric Services*, 1995, 46(6), 569–574.

Ozarin, L. "State Hospitals as Acute Care Facilities." *Hospital and Community Psychiatry*, 1989, 40(1), 5.

Petrila, J. D. "Who Will Pay for Involuntary Civil Commitment Under Capitated Managed Care? An Emerging Dilemma." *Psychiatric Services*, 1995, 46(10), 1045–1048.

Pinheiro, M. V. "Dealing with Managed Care." [http://pw2.netcom/com/~mvp1/soloproviders1.htm]. Sep. 25, 1998.

Rachlin, S., Grossman, S., and Frankel, J. "Patients Without Communities: Whose Responsibility?" *Hospital and Community Psychiatry*, 1979, 30(1), 37–39.

Redick, R., Witkin, M., Atay, J., and Manderscheid, R. *The Evolution and Expansion of Mental Health Care in the United States Between 1955 and 1990*. Mental Health Statistical Note, no. 210. Rockville, Md.: Substance Abuse and Mental Health Services Administration, 1994.

Rothbard, A., and others. "Cost Comparison of State Hospital and Community-Based Care for Seriously Mentally Ill Adults." *American Journal of Psychiatry*, 1998, 155(4), 523–529.

Satel, S. "The Madness of Deinstitutionalization." *Wall Street Journal*, Feb. 20, 1996, p. A18.

Sederer, L., and Summergrad, P. "Criteria for Hospital Admission." *Hospital and Community Psychiatry*, 1993, 44(2) 116–118.

Shapiro, J. "Patients Refused Admission to a Psychiatric Hospital." *Hospital and Community Psychiatry*, 1983, 34(8), 733–736.

Smith, D., Jones, T., and Coye, J. "State Mental Health Institutions in the Next Decade: Illusions and Reality." *Hospital and Community Psychiatry*, 1977, 28(8), 593–597.

Smith, R. "Implementing Psychosocial Rehabilitation with Long-Term Patients in a Public Psychiatric Hospital." *Psychiatric Services*, 1998, 49(5), 593–595.

Sowers, W. "The Ethics of Public Sector Managed Care: Civic Responsibility or Malignant Neglect?" *Community Psychiatrist* (Newsletter of the American Association of Community Psychiatrists), Summer 1995, pp. 1–2.

Spiro, H. "Reforming the State Hospital in a Unified System of Care." *Hospital and Community Psychiatry*, 1982, 33(9), 722–728.

Stratas, N., Bernhardt, D., and Elwell, R. "The Future of the State Mental Hospital: Developing a Unified System of Care." *Hospital and Community Psychiatry*, 1977, 28(8), 598–600.

Strauss, V. "As St. Elizabeths Crumbles, Many Advise Closing It." *Washington Post*, Jan. 23, 1996, p. A1, p. A5.

Sullivan, R. "Hospitals Will Gain by Cutting Bed Use." *New York Times*, Dec. 31, 1979, p. A1, p. A13.

Swidler, R., and Tauriello, J. "New York State's Community Mental Health Reinvestment Act." *Psychiatric Services*, 1995, 46(5), 496–500.

Talbott, J. A. "The Future of Unified Mental Health Services." In J. A. Talbott (ed.), *Unified Mental Health Systems: Utopia Unrealized*. New Directions for Mental Health Services, no. 18. San Francisco: Jossey-Bass, 1983a.

Talbott, J. A. (ed.). *Unified Mental Health Systems: Utopia Unrealized*. New Directions for Mental Health Services, no. 18. San Francisco: Jossey-Bass, 1983b.

Teplin, L. "The Prevalence of Severe Mental Disorder Among Male Urban Jail Detainees: Comparison with the Epidemiologic Catchment Area Program." *American Journal of Public Health*, 1990, 80(6), 663–669.

Thompson, J., and others. "Changing Characteristics of Schizophrenic Patients Admitted to State Hospitals." *Hospital and Community Psychiatry*, 1993, 44(3), 231–235.

Thornicroft, G., and Bebbington, P. "Deinstitutionalisation: From Hospital Closure to Service Development." *British Journal of Psychiatry,* 1989, *155*(1), 739–753.

Torrey, E. "Jails and Prisons: America's New Mental Hospitals." *American Journal of Public Health,* 1995, *85*(12), 1611–1613.

Townsend, E., and Seiden, M., "Structural Inefficiencies at a State Psychiatric Hospital." *Hospital and Community Psychiatry,* 1987, *38*(2), 127–129.

van Norman, J., and Stone, S. Letter to *Psychiatric Services,* 1996, *47*(8), 879.

Warner, R. (ed.). *Alternatives to the Hospital for Acute Psychiatric Treatment.* Washington, D.C.: American Psychiatric Press, 1995.

Wasow, M. "The Need for Asylum Revisited." *Hospital and Community Psychiatry,* 1993, *44*(3), 207–208, 222.

Wilson, W. "Response to Fred W. Becker's 'The Politics of Closing State Mental Hospitals.'" *Community Mental Health Journal,* 1993, *29*(2), 115–117.

Wines, M. "Mental Institutions May Be As Empty As They'll Ever Be." *New York Times,* Sep. 4, 1988, p. E6.

Wing, J. "Planning and Evaluating Services for Chronically Handicapped Psychiatric Patients in the United Kingdom." In L. Stein and M. Test (eds.), *Alternatives to Mental Hospital Treatment.* New York: Plenum, 1975.

Witkin, M., Atay, J., and Manderscheid, R. "Trends in State and County Mental Hospitals in the U.S. from 1970 to 1992." *Psychiatric Services,* 1996, *47*(10), 1079–1081.

Wolpert, J. "Scrooges Among Us." *Washington Post,* June 29, 1995, p. A21.

Wong, D. "Slow Exits at State Mental Hospitals: Recovering Patients Lack Places to Go." *Boston Globe Online,* [http://www.bostonglobe.com]. Mar. 3, 1997.

Zaleski, J., Gale, M., and Winget, C. "Extended Hospital Care as Treatment of Choice." *Hospital and Community Psychiatry,* 1979, *30*(6), 399–401.

Zealberg, J., Santos, A., and Fisher, R. "Benefits of Mobile Crisis Programs." *Hospital and Community Psychiatry,* 1993, *44*(1), 16–17.

Leona L. Bachrach is dean of the William A. Keese School of Continuing Education in Gaithersburg, Maryland. She was formerly research professor of psychiatry (sociology) at the Maryland Psychiatric Research Center of the University of Maryland School of Medicine.

*Many clinicians deny the possibility of violence occurring
in their practices, and this denial has its roots in fear of
violence or overconfidence in safety. To appropriately
address the issue of violence, clinicians must engage in
proactive behaviors and attitudes that will ensure their
safety.*

Clinician Safety: Assessing and Managing the Violent Patient

Arthur Z. Berg, Carl C. Bell, Joe Tupin

Eventually, all relationships must address the issue of aggression, and the
relationship between mental health professional and patient is no different.
Because clinicians frequently choose their profession to relieve suffering and
conceive of the role as nurturing and supportive, a patient's aggression is
frequently a surprise. Many patients who go to clinicians need nurturing
and supportive therapeutic relationships. Unfortunately, many others need
help in controlling behavior that may be excessively aggressive. This being
the case, clinicians must have a thorough understanding about violence and
develop appropriate attitudes regarding various forms of violence (Baker
and Bell, 1999). Although a clinician's mission may be to save lives, lessen
suffering, and do no harm, to fulfill this mission the healer must be safe
from harm.

Denial

A crucial aspect of psychiatric training is learning how to ensure safety. Clinicians therefore need skills in assessing and managing the violent patient.
We often overlook this aspect of psychiatric training or give it minimal
attention. Denial is the primary reason for the lack of institutional concern
that results in ignoring the need for safety training. Denial also plays a role
in clinicians' missing danger signs or overestimating their ability to cope
with potential violence. This denial may have its roots in experiences with
violence or may come from a lack of exposure to violence (Berg, 1997).

The purpose of this chapter is to highlight some paradigmatic principles that should act as guidelines for clinicians who are being attacked or

NEW DIRECTIONS FOR MENTAL HEALTH SERVICES, no. 91, Fall 2001   © John Wiley & Sons, Inc.

confronted by imminently violent and potentially violent patients. The chapter covers issues of personal safety and the management of three levels of violence.

Scope of the Problem

Mental health care providers are at great risk of being attacked by patients.

Prevalence of Violent Incidents in the Mentally Ill. Using National Institute of Mental Health Epidemiologic Catchment Area study data, Swanson, Holzer, Ganju, and Jono (1990) reviewed the incidence of violent behavior during the previous year. They found that the prevalence of violence was five times greater among people who met an Axis I diagnosis than it was among interviewees who were not diagnosable. Furthermore, violence prevalence among persons with a diagnosis of alcoholism or drug abuse was twelve and sixteen times greater, respectively, than it was in subjects who were not diagnosable (Swanson, Holzer, Ganju, and Jono, 1990). It has also been found that co-occurring substance abuse disorder markedly increases the likelihood of violence in patients with a major mental illness, with 31 percent committing at least one act of violence during a one-year follow-up (Steadman and others, 1998). Accordingly, because psychiatry treats patients who have a greater likelihood of perpetrating violence, providing mental health care is a high-risk profession.

Frequency of Assaults on Clinicians. Caretakers and nursing staff are frequent targets of assault. However, physicians are not far behind. The rate of victimization of mental health professionals in the workplace from 1992 to 1996 was 79.5 per 1,000. The rate of victimization of physicians in the workplace from 1992 to 1996 was 15.7 per 1,000 (Bureau of Justice Statistics, 1998). Workplace homicide rates for psychiatrists and mental health professionals are exceeded only by those for taxi drivers, convenience store clerks, and police officers (U.S. Department of Health and Human Services, 1993). Examining the available literature on violence in the health care setting, Tardiff (1987) notes that approximately 40 percent of psychiatrists have been assaulted at some time during their careers, and 48 percent of psychiatric residents are assaulted during residency. In one documented study of eighteen physicians murdered by patients, seven were psychiatrists (Ladds and Lion, 1996). Furthermore, 80 percent of all nurses are assaulted at least once during their careers, resulting in a higher rate of occupational violence than found in any other workplace (Occupational Safety and Health Administration, 1996). Psychiatric nursing staff members experience an even higher rate of assault with more serious injury. Injuries range from bruises to bone fractures and head trauma, and they include rape and homicide. The psychological and economic cost of this workplace violence in mental health settings is staggering. Administrative costs compound the monetary costs of death, injury, and psychological damage. These include lost workdays, staff recruitment and turnover, security, police, investigations, litigation, and workers' compensation.

Many of these assaults are preventable: education and safety training significantly reduce the risk. We must provide safety training quarterly, as we do with cardiopulmonary resuscitation (CPR) and fire drills. Such training must emphasize awareness of risk, principles of managing aggressive behavior, and instruction in self-defense. Like CPR, self-defense instruction must be hands-on and given by qualified instructors.

Personal Safety and Attitudes About Aggression and Violence

When one is confronted with an aggressive, potentially violent patient, personal safety should always be a prime concern. Unfortunately, because of clinician experiences and attitudes, this concern may not be manifest. Clinicians must have appropriate attitudes regarding violence and follow some basic principles to maintain personal safety. Consequently, mental health leadership must place the issue of personal safety in the consciousness of clinicians and emphasize the staff's right to personal safety. Administrators should tell practitioners that they have a right to defend themselves when threatened with bodily harm. Such an assertion removes some potential immobilizing ambivalence or confusion about how to proceed if attacked.

Clinician Experiences with Violence

Once practitioners have openly embraced the value of personal safety, proper supervision and training can correct the hindrances to making them effective and efficient in managing potentially violent patients. In addition, supervision can build on assets in staff to make them more competent and capable of handling violent individuals. Clinician experiences and attitudes may also be a strength in appropriately assessing and treating the violent individual. Practitioners therefore should explore and address those experiences with trauma and violence that might influence their judgment. Clinician exposure to trauma and violence may be quite high. For example, one study of social service providers found that 3 percent reported being physically assaulted, and 7 percent reported being robbed in the past year. Furthermore, 9 percent reported being raped, 11 percent reported being shot at—with 3 percent of these being hit—and 3 percent reported having been stabbed. Regarding witnessing violence, 25 percent reported seeing someone get shot, 25 percent reported seeing someone stabbed, and 11 percent reported seeing someone killed. Finally, 55 percent reported knowing someone who was murdered, and 48 percent reported knowing someone who was raped. Only 3 percent reported ever being counseled (Bell, Mock, and Slutkin, forthcoming).

Hierarchy of Aggression

Exploring clinicians' experiences with violence helps practitioners understand that although violence is aggressive, not all aggression is violent and
therefore aggression requires different approaches. Table 9.1 defines the
hierarchy of aggression further. Having some understanding of this hierarchy helps structure the clinician's response to the various levels of aggression appropriately. Clinicians should understand that hostility may result
from the need to obtain a goal (bullying the doctor to get drugs) or the need
to hurt or destroy anything that frustrates a goal-directed activity such as
self-assertion, exploration, or dominance. Furthermore, hostility may come
from the need to protect oneself from injury (caused by a threat or actual
trauma), and once the perceived injury is addressed, the hostility abates.

Clinician Attitudes

In addition to understanding a hierarchy of aggression, clinicians should
explore their attitudes and affects, as such attitudes and affects influence
patients' responses to mental health professionals. Examples of such attitudes
and affects include being

Table 9.1. Hierarchy of Aggression

1. Lowest level of aggression	1. Alertness, initiative, curiosity, motivation, attentiveness, and exploratory behavior.
2. Self-assertion	2. The attempt to establish, maintain, and expand one's boundaries and integrity while not intruding into others' territory.
3. Dominance	3. The capacity to exert an influence on the behavior of other people or groups in an intended direction (also known as power). Dominance tends to be grounded in coercion— that is, it creates expectation of great rewards or great punishments for certain kinds of behavior.
a. Authority	a. Dominance that is legitimized by legal, professional, or social mores
i. Legitimate	i. Conferred by virtue of a law or formal designation
ii. Charismatic	ii. Bestowed by virtue of having "winning ways with people"
iii. Traditional	iii. Granted out of respect for elders
iv. Mission driven	iv. Accorded by group consensus regarding the purpose of a body
4. Hostility	4. Behavior or attitudes intending to hurt or destroy an object or the self.
a. Violence	a. The use of force to physically injure
5. Hatred	5. The injury or destruction of an object, self, or situation is the end rather than the means to an end.

Source: Parts of this table are adapted from Marcovitz, 1973.

- Fearful, submissive, and excessively permissive
- Brave and overconfident
- Excessively aggressive, controlling, and strict
- Counterphobic
- Detached or avoidant
- Concerned
- Actively friendly (gregarious)
- Passively friendly (helpful but not intrusive)
- Matter-of-fact

Overview of Best Practices

Once clinicians have consciously made an investment in their personal safety, explored their attitudes about violence, and explored their affects toward violent situations, they can pursue best practices to maximize their safety.

Assessment. Assessing the cause of violence is important information that is useful for managing violent patients. Various studies have shown that individuals with certain mental disorders are more likely to be violent than others. These are patients who are

- Withdrawing from drugs or alcohol
- Suffering from chronic organic brain damage resulting in impulsivity
- Suffering from acute organic brain syndromes resulting in deliriousness
- Acutely ill (paranoid patients who feel threatened, manic patients who are agitated, depressed patients who are explosive)
- Suffering from borderline, antisocial, or paranoid personality disorders (Tardiff, 1984; Reid and Balis, 1987)

Consequently, time permitting, management of the violent patient usually begins with special attention to diagnosis.

Timing. Assessment of the cause of violence is facilitated or hindered by the amount of time available. Clearly, while one is being choked is not the time to gather data about why one is being choked. Being choked calls for a physical response. The immediacy of the situation is therefore more important than assessing the cause of violence and is the main principle for managing violence. Therefore we can categorize violence as potential, urgent or imminent, and emergent (Tupin, 1983).

Summary of Best Practices

Managing violence based on the amount of time available to respond is the best practice. Consultation is a critical tool in managing potentially violent patients. Identifying patients with more potential for violence than other patients is also important. Clinician safety also involves awareness of potentially violent situations and settings. Furthermore, clinicians must know how to manage potentially violent patients by maintaining an environmental protective shield and using medication before violence erupts. Clinicians must also be aware of warning signs of escalation leading to imminent violence and must know how to manage imminent violence by de-escalating the imminently violent patient. In addition, if they are unable to de-escalate imminent violence, clinicians need to know how to manage emergent violent behavior using safety and rescue equipment, self-defense, and a coordinated response to violence or assault. Education and training in violence management are critical tools in maintaining clinician safety and should not be overlooked. Finally, reporting violence and assaults and collecting accurate statistics are vitally important if we are to understand the patterns of violence comprehensively.

Potential Violence

Although certain categories of patients are at greater risk for perpetrating violence, as discussed earlier (Swanson, Holzer, Ganju, and Jono, 1990), patients with a history of violence should be considered at an even greater risk for being violent again. Potentially violent patients are individuals who have a history of violence but who are not currently threatening to become violent. In this situation, there is time to plan how to respond to the patient's violence should it manifest itself.

Consultation. Consultation during treatment of violence-prone individuals is crucial and may be lifesaving. Fear, countertransference difficulties, denial, and unrecognized provocative behavior by a therapist or staff member may interfere with good clinical judgment. The therapist and staff may distance themselves from the patient, ignore threats, or overreact and overcontrol. The consultation may be formal or part of ongoing supervision. It may be informal discussion with colleagues, supervisors, or other staff members. It is important that feelings about a patient be discussed. Feelings about a violence-prone patient may include fear, anger, or inappropriate neutrality. In a hospital setting, there should be regularly scheduled staff meetings to discuss violent or potentially violent patients. Staff members should be encouraged to express their feelings. Having such meetings before the admission of violence-prone patients is sometimes useful. This may prevent negative expectations and subsequent distancing by staff. It may prevent overcontrol, which leads to unnecessary use of restraint and seclusion, prolonged length of stay, or excessive use of medication.

Identifying Potentially Violent Patients. Identifying potentially violent individuals is done by obtaining a thorough history of violence (Tardiff, 1984; Reid and Balis, 1987). Such patients can also be identified by conducting background checks through police records for occurrences of assault. Such investigations reveal that some patients are repetitively violent, whereas others have isolated incidents of violence. An important aspect of gathering a history of violence is determining the patient's violence triggers. Research on violent patients reveals that patients with a history of a psychosis who have isolated incidents of violence have their episode of violence while in the throes of an acute decompensation (Mulvey, 1994). Alternatively, patients with a history of a psychosis who have persistent episodes of violence are patients who also have neurological impairment (Krakowski and Czobor, 1994). Fortunately, the standard of violence prediction is not as stringent in real life as it is in the forensic setting. As a result, the clinician can maintain a high index of caution when treating patients with certain diagnoses or problems. A history of violence remains the most reliable predictor of future violence (Brizer, 1989). However, new research based on actuarial data may soon provide tools for predicting potentially violent patients (Hare, 1991; Harris and Rice, 1997).

Awareness of Potentially Violent Situations and Settings. General conditions that increase the risk of harmful assault are

- Alcohol or drug abuse
- Insufficient staff
- Untrained security personnel or lack of emergency devices
- Unsafe architectural layouts, an inability to observe, lack of escape routes
- Furniture or objects that could be used as weapons
- Disquieting or otherwise unpleasant living arrangements for patients or staff

Specific situations that signal an increased risk of violent assault are

- Limit setting with explosive patients—placing in or removing patients from restraints, for example
- Interviewing for fitness to return to duty or discharge from employment
- Interviewing spouses or children in domestic abuse cases
- Being informed that an unfamiliar person has been seen loitering or observing or otherwise appearing at one's home or office
- Having a patient appear at inappropriate times or places
- Receiving unusual phone calls or mail
- Feeling any apprehension or fear that is otherwise unexplainable (De Becker, 1997)

Furthermore, the possibility of having to manage a violent patient is more likely in certain locations than in others. These settings are emergency rooms, crisis clinics, admission units, intensive care units, and detoxification units.

In high-risk situations or settings, mental health professionals should cultivate an increased level of conscious awareness of potentially dangerous situations. Recognizing risk factors for potential violence is a critical skill that aids prevention and safety; therefore a sustained level of alertness is required. This level of alertness, referred to by the police and military as *condition yellow,* is different from having a high index of suspicion or being in red alert. It requires a constant awareness of immediate surroundings—in front, alongside, in back. This is the same level of awareness necessary to drive a car defensively. It is a physiologically healthy, nonparanoid state that enhances the clinical skill of observation. It is neither a totally relaxed nor a hyperalert state, but it is a state of attentiveness to warning signs.

Violent and even lethal confrontations may also occur with dangerous persons not known to the clinician. Mental health professionals may become targets of

- Persons involved in civil or criminal litigation with a patient
- Physical and sexual abusers of patients in treatment
- Spouses or partners of patients in child custody disputes
- Persons with an erotomanic fixation on a patient
- Another clinician's patient who includes others in a delusional system

These persons may perceive the treating or testifying professional as responsible for an undesirable outcome. This can be dangerous. The usual first lines of defense may be insufficient. Hospitalization may not be available. The police and the judicial system may not be able to intervene.

In these instances, there may be warnings such as spoken or written threats or stalking. The following actions should be taken: (1) The clinician should obtain special threat management consultation. Unless police departments or psychiatrists have special expertise in this area, they should not be relied on to assess threats. Experts in this area should be consulted. A coordinated plan with increased security measures may be required. (2) There should be evaluation of the use of restraining orders. However, restraining orders may not suffice or may be contraindicated. Restraining orders may precipitate a violent reaction, as they sometimes do in domestic abuse situations.

There should be no response to any communication, written or spoken, until expert consultation, risk evaluation, and a coordinated security plan have been undertaken. The plan will include appropriate countermeasures. Exact copies and details of all communications should be retained. These are extremely useful to experts in evaluating risk and devising a security plan.

Environmental Protective Shield: Physical and Emotional. Given that some settings are more dangerous than others, creating an environment that prevents violence is an effective approach (Lion, Dubin, and Futrell, 1996; Colling, 1996). By reestablishing a protective shield, previously traumatized individuals will feel safer (Pynoos and Nader, 1988) and less reactive to perceived injury. The setting and previous levels of violence, based on an analysis of incident reports, determine the degree of protective shield needed.

Clinical interviews occur in private offices in homes or commercial buildings where clinicians are solely responsible for their own safety. In these settings, the following precautions should be observed. Patients with a history of violence or paranoia or who are borderline with little impulse control should not be seen here. A more secure setting such as a hospital emergency ward or an office with available psychiatric and security staff is indicated. Although private office comfort and attractiveness are important considerations, complacency and denial should not preclude safety. In addition, a call button that sounds in a reception area or at a neighbor's can be discreetly placed even in the plushest of offices. A small, well-designed one-way mirror may be disguised in a wall or door to check on potentially violent visitors. A spring-locked door that can be closed quickly and securely is useful in handling an unexpected surprise when the waiting room door is opened.

The physical structure of the clinic milieu can also be a great deterrent against violence. Having windows in doors of examining rooms allows privacy while also lending a sense of the possibility of being monitored for unacceptable behavior. Security cameras also provide a sense that behavior is being monitored. Posting rules in the clinic that make it clear that violence will not be tolerated and has consequences is another useful strategy. Preventing areas of relative seclusion from being used for examination purposes can also decrease the use of unmonitored areas that sometimes gives tacit approval for unacceptable behavior. Finally, removing potential weapons, such as scissors, from the clinic office is also a preventive strategy for managing potentially violent patients.

Although offices in emergency rooms and on psychiatric wards should be comfortable and attractive, additional security measures are required. For example, furniture should not block egress and should be heavy or soft so that it cannot be used as a weapon. Similarly, desk and decorative objects such as letter openers and sculptures can be used as weapons. They should not be accessible. In addition, when potentially violent patients are being treated, security personnel may be positioned outside the office door, or clinicians may leave the door open. There should be no spring-loaded locks on these doors. Imminently violent patients may require the presence of other staff or security personnel in the office. In extreme cases, patients may have to be interviewed while in restraints. In addition, a security presence should be visible when patients enter a clinic setting.

Nursing stations and break areas, as well as offices, must be equipped with panic buttons. Personal emergency call devices should be provided to staff members. Restraining equipment, including ambulatory restraints and properly designed seclusion rooms, must be available. Visible restraint cots in psychiatric emergency settings may also send a message that out-of-control behavior is not tolerated. A sense of a protective shield can be established by having patients walk through a portal metal detector or searched before they are examined in an emergency room setting (Bell and Palmer, 1981). Emergency medications should be readily available.

The physical layouts of psychiatric units require specialized planning. Safety features include traffic patterns, patient visibility, and placement of communications and alarms. Access, window construction, and living-area fixtures require special attention. Plate glass can be broken and used as a deadly weapon. Shower heads can be used for suicide attempts or removed and used as weapons. Forensic units and emergency wards have special security needs. They may require magnetometer screening devices to prevent introduction of weapons. They may require increased security personnel, physical barriers, and sophisticated surveillance devices.

The emotional and attitudinal work environment can also prevent violence. Milieus characterized by good teamwork and interdependence present unified fronts against the likelihood of violence. Furthermore, management styles that encourage the establishment and maintenance of good relationships will encourage staff to continue these practices toward patients, and such practices encourage a "connectedness" that has been shown to discourage various violent behaviors (Resnick and others, 1997). Good relationships allow for sensitivity to patients' psychological injuries, which are frequently at the root of violent behavior. Such relationships also help staff in talking a patient down from an agitated, escalating state. Furthermore, such relationships assist in maintaining respect for patient boundaries, the transgression of which may trigger a violent attack.

Uses of Medication in Potentially Violent Patients. Using medication to control target symptoms that promote violence is a useful strategy to prevent violence (Hughes, 1999). For long-term care, medication is often effective in reducing or controlling violence (Tardiff, 1999). Potentially violent patients require careful study to determine if any treatable pathological processes are underlying the violence, and DSM-IV diagnosis (Axes I, II, and III) may be relevant. In particular, note those conditions that have violence as an essential feature, such as intermittent explosive disorder and sexual sadism, and those conditions that have violence as an associated feature, including organic mental disorder and post-traumatic stress disorder (Menninger, 1993). If violence is a direct product of a DSM-IV disorder, medication should be selected to treat that disorder—antipsychotics for schizophrenia-determined violence, for example. However, violence in schizophrenics may also result from coexisting brain injury or substance abuse. In these cases, another medication must be added to the antipsychotic.

Antipsychotics do not have a specific antiviolence effect, and akathisia associated with high-potency medications has been linked to violent behavior. Benzodiazepines have limited application to manage chronic violence. They might be helpful in managing violence linked to anxiety, although a relationship is unstudied. Other antianxiety agents have not been reported to be effective, but buspirone has been noted in case reports to be useful in patients with dementia, traumatic brain injury, and similar conditions. The initial effect may be to increase violence, and the benefit may take several weeks. As central nervous system serotonin availability is thought to be linked to reducing violence, antidepressant medications that increase serotonin are considered useful for the management of chronic violence (Bass and Beltis, 1991; Coccaro, Astill, Herbert, and Schut, 1990; Roy-Byrne and Fann, 1997). Older medications such as trazodone and amitriptyline have been found useful, and patients with brain injury may be good candidates. Antimanic agents such as lithium have been studied in different populations and found effective in conditions other than bipolar disorder, such as brain injury and mental retardation. Those who respond typically are explosive and easily provoked, respond with excessive violence, and may or may not be remorseful (Tupin, 1978). Anticonvulsants have been studied generally in open clinical protocols. Carbamazepine has been reported to be effective for patients with violence and seizures and other organic conditions. Valproic acid has also been used successfully. Antihypertensive medications (beta-blockers), particularly propranolol, have been studied and found useful in patients with organic brain syndromes, although clinical effects may take six to eight weeks.

Imminent Violence

Situations are urgent when patients threaten imminent violence. These situations occur when an individual is escalating and about to commit violence but has not yet acted. In this situation there is some time to intervene but not a great deal of time. Such situations should be easy to identify.

Warning Signs of Imminent Violence. Mental health professionals should be aware of warning signs of imminent violence. Such signs consist of

- Agitated behavior such as pacing
- Threats that are explicit or implicit—spoken, written, or made via gestures
- Body movements, especially of the extremities, such as the opening and closing of fists
- Eye movement and appearance such as dilation or darting
- Proximity, such as when a patient invades a clinician's personal space
- Impulsiveness or the inability to comply with reasonable limit setting
- A recent episode of violent or assaultive behavior
- Fear in the clinician or any otherwise unexplained feeling of apprehension

Warning signs call for action: clinicians are more likely to be harmed when they ignore warning signs because of uncertainty, inexperience, or a false sense of bravado.

Spoken threats are the most frequent warning sign. The context in which a patient makes the threat is the most important factor in assessing the likelihood of aggressive or assaultive behavior. Spoken threats require immediate action when they take place in the following contexts:

- Loud outbursts, name calling, and cursing that are increasing in intensity

- Agitation, pacing, clenching fists
- Drug or alcohol intoxication

These conditions indicate impending loss of control. Immediate de-escalation and other safety measures must be taken. The clinician may have to leave the area. If the verbal content is primarily vulgar and directed at everyone and everything, without an escalation or specific threat, aggressive behavior is still possible but less likely. Spoken threats expressed in a matter-of-fact, unemotional tone can also be dangerous. They require assessment and response, because even though behavior is not escalating, these threats may portend future violence or assault. Threats made in the context of a psychosis are especially dangerous in the presence of

- Agitation
- Suicidal thought or behavior
- Paranoid delusions, particularly those incorporating therapists or staff
- A command voice or other control hallucinations

De-escalation Using Clinical Skills. Observation of behavior that is escalating toward violence calls for an immediate verbal intervention designed to calm the patient down and de-escalate the situation from urgent or imminent to potential. The ability to de-escalate and "calm down" an agitated or threatening person is therefore basic for all clinicians (Walker, 1983). Usually, using interpersonal-relationship skills to quickly establish a relationship or to build on an existing relationship is a useful strategy. Making it clear to the patient that the clinician is empathic toward the patient and wants to help the patient address the source of agitation or anger is necessary for a win-win outcome. Problem solving with the patient on how to address the source of agitation or anger will empower the patient and decrease the injury generating the anger. De-escalating has three components:

- Verbal—what is said and how it is said, both of which are critical
- Space—respecting the patient's sense of personal space
- Body language—nonthreatening positions, gestures, and movements

With an emotionally escalating patient, the object of verbal intervention is to decrease the patient's underlying feelings of fear, inadequacy, and hopelessness. Volume, tone, and rate of speech should be lower than the patient's (although if they are too low, the patient may perceive it as a threat). Assure the patient that he or she is understood. The patient should be listened to actively, with sufficient, nonintimidating eye contact. Statements should paraphrase the patient's statements to underscore that he or she is understood. All statements must be honest and precise. If not, they may encourage increased escalation. The goal is to encourage the patient to model the clinician's behavior and have a calmer interaction. Redirection of the conversation to less charged subjects may be helpful occasionally. Verbal limit setting, but not in an authoritative threatening manner, may be appropriate. Explain the rules of the milieu or the real consequences of the behavior. The fact that the behavior is frightening to you and others should be expressed. It may help decrease the patient's fear. Suggestions for increasing the patient's sense of safety include moving to a less threatening area; assuming seated, less threatening positions; and offering food or drink.

An escalating patient's personal space must be respected. When patients are agitated or threatened, their perceived zone of personal space increases, as does the fear of its being invaded. This personal space can be visualized as an oval zone extending four to six feet all around. Intrusion into that space will increase fear and thus the likelihood of assault. Remaining outside the oval zone of personal space also allows the clinician time to react to any assault. Approaching an escalating person should be made from the front or side, as an approach from behind is extremely threatening. The clinician should never turn his or her back to the agitated or threatening patient.

As a patient's hospital room or living area may be regarded as personal space, request permission before entering. Escape routes, for the patient and the clinician, must not be blocked. If possible, the de-escalation should take place away from other patients or any atmosphere likely to overstimulate. Other staff should be present to assist, if necessary.

A show of force is sometimes necessary and may effectively preclude the need to escalate to physical restraint. The aggressive person will frequently capitulate in the presence of perceived overwhelming odds. A show of force may also increase the patient's sense of safety and control. If a show of force is employed, the patient must not be made to feel cornered or that his or her personal space is invaded.

The agitated, escalating patient is extremely sensitive to body language. The clinician's general demeanor, including posture and movements, is important. Nonaggressive stances and gestures are perceived as less threatening. They are also powerful tools for getting the patient to model the clinician's calmer attitude. One example of a nonthreatening position is to hold the hands at waist level with the palms up and open. The Thinker stance (one forearm crosses the chest, the opposite elbow rests on it, with the index finger of that hand on the cheek or chin) is also nonthreatening. Any position that makes the clinician appear smaller, thus less threatening, is the object. Do not touch the patient or startle him or her with sudden movement, even to reassure. The clinician's body should be at a forty-five-degree angle to the disturbed patient. This keeps more of the clinician's body out of personal space and allows a larger reactionary gap in case of sudden assault. It also permits better balance and position if defensive or evasive movement is needed.

The ability to de-escalate requires practice in training situations. It requires practice to withstand an intense verbal barrage with a calm demeanor. It requires training to learn when a de-escalation should not be attempted. In some instances, it may be good clinical judgment to leave the area.

De-escalation Using Medication. Urgent situations will benefit from sedating medications for short-term control of violence. Short-term control of imminent violence by medication relies on the sedative effects of sedative benzodiazepines or high-potency neuroleptics (Tardiff, 1999). An agitated or imminently violent patient may accept oral medication instead of an injection. Haloperidol is a commonly used and effective drug. It is administered in five-milligram doses intramuscularly (IM) or via a slow-push intravenous line (IV). The dose may be repeated every twenty to thirty minutes as needed. If the patient has not responded after two doses, benzodiazepine may be added. This combination is usually effective and may have fewer side effects than higher doses of either drug alone. Lorazepam is a preferred benzodiazepine because it may be given intramuscularly or by slow-push IV (Saltzman and others, 1991). It may be administered alone or in combination with haloperidol, as above. The dose is one or two milligrams every twenty to thirty minutes until the patient is calm. Deeper sedation is usually not required or desirable. The effectiveness of these medications is not an indication for their long-term use. Administration of either of these two types of medications should be limited to a few weeks unless a specific diagnosis is identified that justifies continuation. They should be discontinued once the crisis subsides. Long-term medication, if any, is dependent on the underlying psychiatric or medical diagnosis. Drugs used for long-term management of aggressive or violent behaviors are usually not effective in emergencies. Causing a paradoxical disinhibition syndrome is rare for benzodiazepines. If the patient has a known history of that reaction, a neuroleptic is used. If the patient is agitated or violent as a result of alcohol withdrawal or is known to have a seizure history, neuroleptics are avoided. They might lower seizure thresholds. Haloperidol, although safe, has not been approved by the Food and Drug Administration for IV use. Restricting that use to settings with monitoring capability, such as hospital units and emergency wards, is best.

Emergent Violence

Emergent violence occurs when patients are being overtly violent. When the patient's violence is emerging, there is no time to prevent violence. This is a time for escape. This is a time for calling for help. This is a time for restraining the patient, guided by a coordinated response. In more critical situations, self-defense may be appropriate. Emergent situations call for the nonspecific sedating effects of either antipsychotics or benzodiazepines, following the guidelines described previously, except that parenteral administration will often be required.

With emergent violence, there is no time to plan, and the intervention has to be physical in nature. If one is attacked by an assailant who does not have a weapon, a good strategy is to clinch, or bear hug, the individual the same way boxers do when they get into trouble in the ring. Just hold on as tight and close as possible and let patients tire themselves out (watch out for biting). This is also a good strategy even if the individual is using a striking weapon such as a club or a chair.

Once a physical attack has been spent, it is a good idea to restrain the patient or put the patient in restraints. Ideally, five people should help restrain a patient. However, in the event there are not enough people, and patient violence is dangerous, self-defense strategies and joint immobilization techniques may be necessary. The bigger the area in which the restraining occurs the better. Aikido training is probably the best martial art to study to become an expert in restraining patients (Westbrook and Ratti, 1974; Tohei, 1975).

Once violence has occurred and the crisis is over, the staff needs to do an autopsy to understand what happened, debrief to reduce tension of those involved, and plan how to respond more effectively, if possible. Critical incident debriefing is a standardized, easily learned technique that can be used to help staff recover from workplace violence. Incident reports need to be filled out and reviewed regularly to detect any weaknesses in the management of violent individuals.

Safety and Rescue Equipment. Physical restraint devices, for restraining two or all four extremities, should be available in psychiatric and emergency department settings. Posey torso devices can accomplish restraint in a bed or a chair. Ambulatory restraints, such as protective aggression devices, can prevent arm strikes yet allow the patient to walk about (Maier, Van Rybroek, and Mays, 1994). The devices can be adjusted and tethered to control extent of movement.

Seclusion rooms are a safety device to protect staff from violent patients. They also provide the patient with a sense of safety and control. Seclusion areas must be scrupulously designed to avoid any danger. They must be constructed so patients cannot pull up floorboards, plaster sections, nails, or other dangerous materials. As violent patients may be suicidal, lighting and electrical outlets must not be accessible. There can be no structure or fixture on which a patient might hang himself or herself.

Having a written protocol for use of restraints and seclusion is essential. It is equally important that staff have adequate training in their use. The greatest number of staff injuries occurs during the placing and removing of physical restraints and during patient takedowns with and without the use of a blanket or mattress. These events also account for the largest incidence of patient injuries.

Nonlethal sprays are effective safety and rescue devices. Hospital security staff use them. They can subdue otherwise unmanageable assaultive behavior, deter without needing to be discharged, and effect rescue in emergency hostage situations. Oleoresin capsicum (OC), or pepper spray, is effective. Mace, omega-chloracephenone (CN), and tear gas are not effective as they have delayed reaction time and are potentially dangerous. Their use is for crowd control. Use of nonlethal sprays by psychiatric staff, as opposed to security personnel, is controversial. However, emergencies cannot always wait for security personnel.

Clinicians have the option of carrying an OC device in their private practices and off duty. Certification in its use requires only a two-hour course.

Self-Defense. We cannot always anticipate or prevent violent, harmful, or lethal assault. In these rare events, we may require spontaneous reaction to survive. Complacency and denial usually result in fatality. As with anticipated assaults, the responsible clinician will have a prearranged plan. That plan could include brief professional instruction or lectures in self-defense. We cannot effectively learn reflexive defensive reactions from a book. Courses and lectures are useful for clinicians of both sexes and of all ages and physical conditions.

In an anticipated attack, a few deep, slow breaths decrease anxiety and provide a moment to prepare. In unanticipated attack, holding one's breath, a usual reaction to acute stress or panic, promotes "freezing" and diminishes clarity, strength, and endurance. We can visualize defensive reaction scenarios for most settings in professional and private life. This also helps reduce the freeze reaction should the unthinkable happen. A most important fundamental is that effective self-defense requires a predetermined decision that an all-out effort will be made until the attacker is incapacitated, help arrives, or there is a completely safe method of escape. The idea of harming someone is foreign to most mental health workers. Nonviolent methods that do not cause harm are appropriate for management of aggressive patients. But when one is faced with serious bodily injury or death, those methods may not apply. The clinician must be prepared to do whatever violence is necessary to save himself or herself and others. In these situations, "First, do no harm" has no place.

Coordinated Response to Violence and Assault. Psychiatric facilities should have a written protocol that addresses

Responding to overt violence, de-escalating impending violence, and flagging potentially violent patients (the latter is especially useful with computerized records)

Identifying warning signs of impending violence

Responding to specific indications with coordinated methods, usually through a designated staff team that is skilled and practiced in managing overtly violent patients (de-escalation, escort techniques, use of restraining devices, patient control with use of blankets or a mattress, and proper show-of-force procedures)

Education and training in understanding violence, violence safety, and self-defense

Policies and practices for maintaining safe environments

A quality assurance system designed to monitor violence and take corrective action

Emphasis should be on

• Decreasing disquieting or otherwise unpleasant environments for patients and staff

- Establishing a solid rapport with the patient
- Using medication to prevent violence
- Respecting the patient's sense of space and value
- Developing a plan with the family member for safety and intervention
- Warning individuals about dangerous patients
- Ensuring that interview rooms are safe
- Ensuring a sense of security in the clinical setting
- Developing a plan to manage patients with weapons

Agency security personnel must be well trained in the management of aggressive behavior (Maier, 1996). Security personnel and the staff response team should function as a coordinated unit with everybody—physicians included—practicing drills (Colling, 1995).

As part of the coordinated response, the administration must promote training, collect statistical data, and provide support to involved staff or visitors. The administration may need to deal with potential litigation or treatment plans that call for prosecution of a patient who has threatened or assaulted. The administration is also responsible for developing standard operating procedures on how to manage various levels of aggression and violence. Such procedures should detail how to manage violence, access emergency medical treatment, make a police report and press charges, file incident reports, and debrief staff involved with violent incidents.

A coordinated response plan and drills based on realistic scenarios add to clinician safety. However, the most effective team response effort and well-constructed protocol cannot negate one reality: the ultimate responsibility for safety remains with the individual clinician.

Education and Training

All clinicians should have mandatory, recurrent education about violence safety during training, during early career years, and as a part of continuing education throughout their careers. Formal presentations such as lectures and seminars should address these topics:

Evaluation, differential diagnosis, and psychodynamics of violence. We should stress the importance of thorough history taking. Information obtained from outside sources is essential, particularly information about past violent behavior. Information about violent or sexual fantasies is important.

Standards and procedures for emergencies. Clinicians should understand use of communications, alarms such as panic buttons, restraint and seclusion protocols, and liability issues.

Consultation. In psychotherapy, pharmacotherapy, and group and milieu therapy, transference issues may lead to poor results and possibly unrecognized danger.

Education. Physicians should have additional education in psychopharmacology of aggressive and violent behavior, forensic issues of consent, involuntary commitment, treatment refusal, and duty to warn.

Training. Mandatory, recurrent education must include training in safety skills. These skills should be practiced in realistically simulated exercises under the supervision of qualified instructors. Training should be augmented with demonstration and audiovisual aids. Skills should include the following: de-escalating aggressive behavior, physical management of aggressive behavior, recognition of and response to dangerous situations, and basic self-defense techniques.

Reporting of Violence and Assaults

The high rate of violence and assault on mental health clinicians is a serious problem, yet studies indicate the number of assaults is underreported by a factor of five (Dubin and Lion, 1996). Accurate statistics play a crucial role in planning for increased clinician safety, and accuracy requires a uniform system of incident reporting. One difficulty in obtaining accurate statistics is the lack of uniformity in defining violence, assault, or aggression and the lack of uniform measures of severity. The following considerations could enhance clinician safety:

Identification of facilities or specific factors that result in higher assault and violence rates. These might include admission and staffing policies, better staff and security personnel training, and physical plant or protocol changes.

Identification of special categories of mental health clinicians at increased risk. These could include specialty area and work location and could include specific clinicians. Psychiatric residents and early-career psychiatrists, for example, are at increased risk.

Identification of certain behaviors or personality traits that may be predisposed to assault. Some personality factors, such as increased irritability in psychiatric residents, are associated with multiple assaults.

Identification of patient categories and individual patients with a greater likelihood of violence and assault. This could increase the effectiveness of flagging violence-prone patients to protect ward staff and individual clinicians better. It would greatly enhance epidemiological study of violence-prone individuals. It could underscore the significance of recidivism, as it is estimated that only 5 percent of patients cause 90 percent of violent assaults.

Documentation of the most serious assaults, such as rape and homicide.

Identification of the extent and severity of clinician danger. This would help overcome inertia among institutions, professional associations, and individuals in regard to addressing this extensive, extremely important problem.

Conclusions

Several factors contribute to inertia about clinician safety: individual institutions do not want to be seen as having problems. Professional associations do not want to stigmatize mental health patients further, and they may give higher priority to other political concerns than to the safety of their members. Individual clinicians may believe that violence and assault are part of the job or have feelings of guilt over such incidents. Always the overriding factor is a psychological denial of the fear of violence.

Recommendations

All clinicians should receive training on how to manage violent patients.

Training review committees should be asked to consider the necessity for clinicians to be knowledgeable about violence.

Recertification examinations should include an assessment of clinicians' knowledge about managing violent patients.

Clinicians should be encouraged to collaborate with appropriate organizations concerning violent patients—prisons, jails, juvenile justice systems, probation offices, forensic hospitals, and community schools.

References

Baker, F. M., and Bell, C. C. "African-American Treatment Concerns." *Psychiatric Services*, 1999, *50*(3), 362–368.

Bass, J. N., and Beltis, J. "Therapeutic Effect of Fluoxetine on Naltrexone-Resistant Self-Injurious Behavior in an Adolescent with Mental Retardation." *Journal of Child and Adolescent Pharmacology*, 1991, *1*, 331–340.

Bell, C. C., Mock, L., and Slutkin, G. "Prevalence of Victimization and Perception of Job Neighborhood Safety in Social Service Staff and the Need for Screening." *Journal of the National Medical Association,* forthcoming.

Bell, C. C., and Palmer, J. M. "Security Procedures in a Psychiatric Emergency Service." *Journal of the National Medical Association,* 1981, *73*(9), 835–842.

Berg, A. "Survival and the Ultimate Threat." *Psychiatric Times,* 1997, *14*(6), 33–36.

Brizer, D. A. "Introduction: Overview of Current Approaches to the Prediction of Violence." In D. A. Brizer and M. Crowner (eds.), *Current Approaches to the Prediction of Violence.* Washington D.C.: American Psychiatric Press, 1989.

Bureau of Justice Statistics. *Special Report: National Crime Victimization Survey, Workplace Violence, 1992–96.* NCJ 168634. Washington, D.C.: U.S. Department of Justice, Office of Justice Programs, July 1998.

Coccaro, E. F., Astill, J. L., Herbert, J. L., and Schut, A. G. "Fluoxetine Treatment of Impulsive Aggression in DSM-III-R Personality Disorder Patients." *Journal of Clinical Psychopharmacology*, 1990, *10*(5), 373–375.

Colling, R. L. *Basic Training Manual for Healthcare Security Officers.* Lombard, Ill.: International Association for Healthcare Security and Safety, 1995.

Colling, R. L. *Keeping the Healthcare Environment Safe.* Oakbrook Terrace, Ill.: Joint Commission on Accreditation of Healthcare Organizations, 1996.

De Becker, G. *The Gift of Fear: Survival Signals That Protect Us from Violence.* New York: Little, Brown, 1997.

Dubin, W. R., and Lion, J. R. "Violence Against the Medical Profession." In J. R. Lion, W. R. Dubin, and D. E. Futrell (eds.), *Creating a Secure Workplace.* Chicago: American Hospital Publishing, 1996.

Hare, R. D. *The Psychopathy Checklist—Revised.* Toronto: Multi-Health Systems, 1991.

Harris, G. T., and Rice, M. E. "Risk Appraisal and Management of Violent Behavior." *Psychiatric Services,* 1997, *48,* 1–9.

Hughes, D. H. "Acute Psychopharmacological Management of the Aggressive Psychotic Patient." *Psychiatric Services,* 1999, *50*(9), 1135–1137.

Krakowski, M. I., and Czobor, P. "Clinical Symptoms, Neurological Impairment, and Prediction of Violence in Psychiatric Inpatients." *Hospital and Community Psychiatry,* 1994, *45,* 700–705.

Ladds, B., and Lion, J. R. "Severe Assaults and Homicide Within Medical Institutions." In J. R. Lion, W. R. Dubin, and D. E. Futrell (eds.), *Creating a Secure Workplace.* Chicago: American Hospital Publishing, 1996.

Lion, J. R., Dubin, W. R., and Futrell, D. E. (eds.). *Creating a Secure Workplace.* Chicago: American Hospital Publishing, 1996.

Maier, G. J. "Training Security Staff in Aggression Management." In J. R. Lion, W. R. Dubin, and D. E. Futrell (eds.), *Creating a Secure Workplace.* Chicago: American Hospital Publishing, 1996.

Maier, G. J., Van Rybroek, G. J., and Mays, D. V. "A Report on Staff Injuries and Ambulatory Restraints: Dealing with Patient Aggression." *Journal of Psychosocial Nursing and Mental Health Services,* 1994, *32*(11), 23–29.

Marcovitz, E. "Aggression in Human Adaptation." *Psychoanalytic Quarterly,* 1973, *42,* 226–232.

Menninger, W. W. "Management of the Aggressive and Dangerous Patient." *Bulletin of the Menninger Clinic,* 1993, *57,* 208–217.

Mulvey, E. P. "Assessing the Evidence of a Link Between Mental Illness and Violence." *Hospital and Community Psychiatry,* 1994, *45,* 663–668.

Occupational Safety and Health Administration. *Guidelines for Preventing Workplace Violence for Health Care and Social Service Workers.* OSHA 3148. Washington, D.C.: U.S. Department of Labor, 1996.

Pynoos, R., and Nader, K. "Psychological First Aid for Children Who Witness Community Violence." *Journal of Traumatic Stress,* 1988, *1*(4), 445–473.

Reid, W. H., and Balis, G. U. "Evaluation of the Violent Patient." In R. E. Hales and A. J. Frances (eds.), *Psychiatric Update: The American Psychiatric Association Annual Review.* Vol. 6. Washington, D.C.: American Psychiatric Press, 1987.

Resnick, M. D., and others. "Protecting Adolescents from Harm: Findings from the National Longitudinal Study on Adolescent Health." *Journal of the American Medical Association,* 1997, *278*(10), 823–832.

Roy-Byrne, P. P., and Fann, J. R. "Psychopharmacologic Treatments for Patients with Neuropsychiatric Disorders." In S. C. Yudofsky and R. E. Hales (eds.), *The American Psychiatric Press Textbook of Neuropsychiatry.* (3rd ed.) Washington, D.C.: American Psychiatric Press, 1997.

Saltzman, C., and others. "Parenteral Lorazepam Versus Parenteral Haloperidol for the Control of Psychiatric Disruptive Behavior." *Journal of Clinical Psychiatry,* 1991, *52,* 177–180.

Steadman, H. J., and others. "Violence by People Discharged from Acute Psychiatric Inpatient Facilities and by Others in the Same Neighborhoods." *Archives of General Psychiatry,* 1998, *55,* 393–401.

Swanson, J. W., Holzer, C. E., Ganju, V. K., and Jono, R. T. "Violence and Psychiatric Disorder in the Community: Evidence from the Epidemiologic Catchment Area Surveys." *Hospital and Community Psychiatry,* 1990, *41,* 761–770.

Tardiff, K. (ed.). *The Psychiatric Uses of Seclusion and Restraint.* Washington, D.C.: American Psychiatric Press, 1984.

Tardiff, K. "Determinants of Human Violence." In R. E. Hales and A. J. Frances (eds.), *Psychiatric Update: The American Psychiatric Association Annual Review.* Vol. 6. Washington, D.C.: American Psychiatric Press, 1987.

Tardiff, K. "Violence." In R. E. Hales, S. C. Yudofsky, and J. A. Talbott (eds.), *The American Psychiatric Press Textbook of Psychiatry.* (3rd ed.) Washington, D.C.: American Psychiatric Press, 1999.

Tohei, K. *This Is Aikido.* Tokyo: Japan Publications, 1975.

Tupin, J. P. "Usefulness of Lithium for Aggression." *American Journal of Psychiatry,* 1978, *135,* 1118.

Tupin, J. P. "The Violent Patient: A Strategy for Management and Diagnosis." *Hospital and Community Psychiatry,* 1983, *34,* 37–40.

U.S. Department of Health and Human Services. *Fatal Injuries to Workers in the United States, 1980–1989: A Decade of Surveillance.* Washington, D.C.: U.S. Department of Health and Human Services, Public Health Service, Centers for Disease Control and Prevention, National Institute for Occupational Safety and Health, 1993.

Walker, J. I. *Psychiatric Emergencies: Intervention and Resolution.* Philadelphia: Lippincott, 1983.

Westbrook, A., and Ratti, O. *Aikido and the Dynamic Sphere.* Rutland, Vt.: Charles E. Tuttle, 1974.

ARTHUR Z. BERG *is assistant professor of psychiatry at Harvard Medical School and Massachusetts General Hospital. He is also a certified instructor in threat management and personal defense and a member of the American Society of Law Enforcement Trainers.*

CARL C. BELL *is professor of psychiatry and public health at the University of Illinois at Chicago and chief executive officer and president of the Community Mental Health Council and Foundation in Chicago.*

JOE TUPIN *is professor emeritus of psychiatry at the University of California, Davis, and medical director emeritus at the University of California, Davis, Medical Center*

INDEX

SINGLE ISSUE SALE

For a limited time save 10% on single issues! Save an additional 10% when you purchase three or more single issues. Each issue is normally 28^{00}.

Please see the next page for a complete listing of available back issues.

Mail or fax this completed form to: Jossey-Bass, A Wiley Company
350 Sansome Street • Fifth Floor • San Francisco CA 94104-1342

CALL OR FAX

Phone 888-378-2537 or 415-433-1740 *or Fax* 800-605-2665 or 415-433-4611 (*attn customer service*)
BE SURE TO USE PROMOTION CODE DF3 TO GUARANTEE YOUR DISCOUNT!
Please send me the following issues at 25^{20} each.

(Important: please include series initials and issue number, such as MHS88)

1. MHS _____

_____

_____

$ _____ Total for single issues (25^{20} each)

_____ Less 10% if ordering 3 or more issues

_____ Shipping charges: Up to $30, add 5^{50} • 30^{01} –$50, add 6^{50} 50^{01} –$75, add 7^{50} • 75^{01} –$100, add 9^{00} • 100^{01} –$150, add 10^{00}
Over $150, call for shipping charge

$ _____ Total (Add appropriate sales tax for your state. Canadian residents add GST)

❏ Payment enclosed (U.S. check or money order only)

❏ VISA, MC, AmEx Discover Card #_____ Exp. date _____

Signature _____ Day phone

❏ Bill me (U.S. institutional orders only. Purchase order required)

Purchase order #_____

Name _____

Address _____

_____

Phone _____ E-mail _____

For more information about Jossey-Bass, visit our website at: www.josseybass.com

OFFER EXPIRES FEBRUARY 28, 2002.   **PRIORITY CODE = DF3**

Other Titles Available in the New Directions for Mental Health
Services Series
H. Richard Lamb, Editor-in-Chief